RELATIONAL

ACUITY 5.0

Downloading Kingdom Intelligence

Tiffany Buckner

Relational Acuity 5.0
Downloading Kingdom Intelligence

©2022, Tiffany Buckner
www.tiffanybuckner.com
info@tiffanybuckner.com

Published by Anointed Fire House

Edited by:
Anointed Fire House
J. Junga
Mr. Accurate Editing

ISBN: 978-1-955557-31-3

Unless otherwise noted, Scripture quotations are taken from The Holy Bible, New King James Version® (NKJV). Copyright© 1982 by Thomas Nelson. Used by permission. All rights reserved. Scriptures taken from the NEW AMERICAN STANDARD BIBLE®,

TABLE OF CONTENTS

INTRODUCTION

The do's, the don'ts, the how's, where's and the when's ...
we haven't been taught to question what we've accepted
as the norms of society, and because of this, a lot of us
rob ourselves of one of the greatest treasures that anyone
can have, and that is healthy, Godly relational acumen. In
truth, most people have never even been introduced to
this phrase, so we build culturally accepted relationships,
rather than building Kingdom relationships. What you'll
find is that most relationships are dysfunctional because
the people in those relationships are not functioning at
their God-capacities. By this, I mean that they don't truly
know YAHWEH; consequently, they don't know themselves
or their own potential. And what we have a tendency to do
is supplement our lack of a relationship with and revelation
of God with a myriad of dysfunctional human
relationships, not realizing that every God-instituted
relationship has a function! The problem is that we tend to
pervert the purposes of those relationships because no one
has ever taught us how to have multidimensional
relationships! All the same, our human relationships mirror
our relationships with God! This is because the large
majority of mankind lacks Kingdom intelligence.

Relational Acuity 5.0 (Downloading Kingdom Intelligence) is
a world of revelation written to help you form, build and
sustain healthy, Godly and productive relationships that
are mutually beneficial and multidimensional. In this
powerful guide, you will also learn how to better categorize
all of your relationships; this way, you can maximize the
potential of each relationship and become an even greater
blessing to the people God entrusts you with. The finale in

the Relational Acuity book series, 5.0 was written to help you understand the problems that arise in many relationships; it is a book of language, a book of direction and, most importantly, a book of revelation. You don't have to spend the rest of your life feeling alone, insecure, misunderstood or mismanaged; you simply need to grow your relational acuity, and this powerful book series will help you to do just that! But buyer beware, the revelation in this book is so potent that it will force you to take inventory of your relationships, and what you may discover is that the reason you've been experiencing delay or what the Bible refers to as "hope deferred" is because you've allowed the enemy to surround you with the wrong people or you've allowed him to pervert your relationships with the right people, but not anymore! After you read this powerful and well-written book, your life will never be the same!

WHEN WORLDS PARALLEL

Imagine driving a car with an eight-year old in the passenger's seat. To avoid the awkward silence, you try to strike up a conversation with the child. "How was school today?" you ask. The child looks down at his knees as if there is something on his leg. "I don't know," he says. What does he mean that he doesn't know how school was? He was there! Nevertheless, you have to remind yourself that you're talking to someone who is eight years removed from the womb, meaning he's still somewhat of a foreigner to the world he's in. "Did you learn anything? Did you do anything fun?" You look at the kid hoping that this new line of questioning will help to break the ice. Once again, he stares at his knees, and then out the window. He then shrugs his shoulders and lets out an exaggerated sigh. "Okay, so let's try this. What's your teacher's name?" you ask. Realizing that you are persistent, the little boy finally answers. "Her name is now Mrs. Winters. She was Mrs. Dynasty, but she said that life changed her name to Mrs. Winters." Life? What does he mean by that? "Do you care to explain? Did she just get married?" you ask as you pull up to the kid's favorite restaurant. Seeing the golden arches, the little boy's excitement becomes evident. Howbeit, he hurriedly answers your question so that he can focus on excitedly talking about what he wants to talk about, and that is food! "She just got a divorce," he says as he fumbles with his backpack. "I think that he put her in jail for a long time because she told our principal that she's

1

glad to be free."

What's happening here? While you are sharing the same space with an eight-year old, the truth is that you guys are in two totally different worlds. Notice I didn't say that you were both on different planets; I said that you were in two worlds. The word "world" doesn't necessarily reference planets every time it's used. In this (and many other cases), it's used to reference systems. What is a system? Oxford Languages gives two definitions of the word "system." They are:
- a set of things working together as parts of a mechanism or an interconnecting network.
- a set of principles or procedures according to which something is done; an organized framework or method.

For example, a surgeon has a world. The same is true for beauticians, politicians, clothing designers and every profession underneath the sun. Each world has a category of information allotted to it, and this information is divided up into sectors and levels. Some people have access to more information than others; this is largely because of their ranks, tenures and sacrifices in those systems. The best way to explain this is—the child has access to the revelation that's being fed to him by his parents, his family members, his teachers, his peers and everyone who has access to him. The children in his life have a severe lack of information because they too are children, so his main diet consists mostly of the information being fed to him by the adults in his life. All the same, the adults have to intentionally withhold some of what they know from him, only feeding him the information that he is mature enough to process and understand. What this means is that his revelational diet is incredibly limited. Your world or your diet, on the other hand, is filled with the knowledge, experiences and understanding that you've acquired over the course of your life. Because of this, the two of you are in different worlds. You've been to his world before, so you know how to address and respond to him, but he's never been in your world. This means that you can lower yourself to communicate with him, but he cannot effectively elevate himself to communicate with you on your level. Now, imagine the person sitting next to you being a woman who is the same age as you. Does this necessarily mean that she's in the same space mentally and emotionally as you are? Of course not. Your worldview may parallel hers, and vice versa. This is because each world can be likened to a mountain. The bottom is bigger and more populated than the top, therefore, each person's worldview will be largely determined by the level on which he or she stands. Imagine standing at the top of a mountain, watching a pride of lions approaching the folks at the bottom of the mountain. The problem is that the lions are hiding in the bushes, crouching and slowly approaching the people whenever they are distracted. What's distracting them? The activity that's taking place on the levels that they are yet to ascend to. Imagine screaming at those people in an attempt to warn them about the impending danger. Nevertheless, someone at the bottom of the mountain uses his walkie to respond. He says to you, "I don't see any lions! You're making this up because you don't want to be held accountable for causing it to rain on us all of yesterday." You pick up your walkie and respond. "Sir, as I've told you before in times past, I don't have the ability to make it rain. I would try to prove my point to you, but I'm calling down to warn you that there is a large pride of lions not too far away from you all, and they are crouching behind bushes and trees. Please retreat to your caves." The man laughs, grabs his microphone and says to the audience of people at the bottom, "She wants us to believe that we're about to be eaten by a bunch of lions! Wait! If that's not funny enough, she wants us to believe that she didn't shake the skies on yesterday, causing it to rain all over us!" The people begin to roar with laughter. "Is she serious?!" one man exclaims as he falls to the ground laughing. A woman towards the east of the crowd follows suit, "She thinks we're stupid because we're down here and she's up there! What a moron!" The crowd continues to hurl insults and laugh; that is until they are attacked by the lions. What happened here? The people were swallowed up because of their worldviews. They were warned by someone who had a greater vantage than themselves, but their pride and ignorance would not allow them to honor you because they could not relate to:

- The journey you've taken to get where you are.
- The price you've paid to get where you are.
- The sacrifices you've made to get where you are.
- Your worldviews.

They lived in the same world or system as you. They could see you and you could see them. They could hear you and you could hear them. They looked like you and you looked like them. Howbeit, your worldviews were not the same. The same is true for that eight-year old boy riding next to you. While the two of you can clearly see one another, the fact of the matter is your worldviews are different because he hasn't lived as long as you've lived, he hasn't gone to the places you've gone, he hasn't experienced nearly as much as you've experienced, and therefore, he doesn't know everything you know. As a matter of fact, he doesn't have access to all of the information and revelation that you have access to. Then again, whatever information he does have access to, he doesn't have a firm enough foundation of knowledge to place that information on, meaning, he can become knowledgeable but he won't understand everything he knows.

Every time God gives you access to more revelation and information, He is inviting you into a new season, after all, a season is a space of time that you are within the confines or limitations of a certain measure of information. It's when God illuminates, for example, a certain percentage of the world you're in, thus allowing you to see and utilize the tools and mysteries of that world. This means that each world has a measure of darkness (ignorance) and light (revelation). Think of it this way. Imagine you're flying above one hundred miles of acreage, and as you navigate that dark space, you see measures of light, from small to great. In each measure or pocket of light, you see one or more people. You fly across cities filled with light and you fly above lights so dim that they almost look like night lights. Cities of light are spaces and places that host wise people; dimmer spaces are places that are inhabited by slaves, but get this, these people aren't the slaves of other people. They are the slaves of comfort. They are comfortable and content with the minute measures of information they have, and even when God illuminates greater spaces around them, they refuse to move too far outside of their comfort zones because they fear and abhor change. Nevertheless, the ones who have the least amount of light (revelation) are the loudest and most demanding people. They want what they see the other "city folks" enjoying, but they don't want to leave their comfort zones to acquire the things or the realities they are lusting after. Now, imagine being a person who has made the journey and given the sacrifices to ascend to new levels, and imagine your best friend riding alongside you in your car. What will your conversation sound like? In truth, if she's never been to the world you're in, she will repeatedly bring you back to the world you've come out of. This means that you will have to lower yourself to speak with her. Now, don't get me wrong. I'm not saying that you should abandon her. What I am saying is, you need people to walk with you who share your worldviews. That friend may have been your best friend in times past, but today, the two of you have very little in common. Consequently, it may be time for her to transition from your intimate circle into your intellectual circle. As a reminder, look at the following chart.

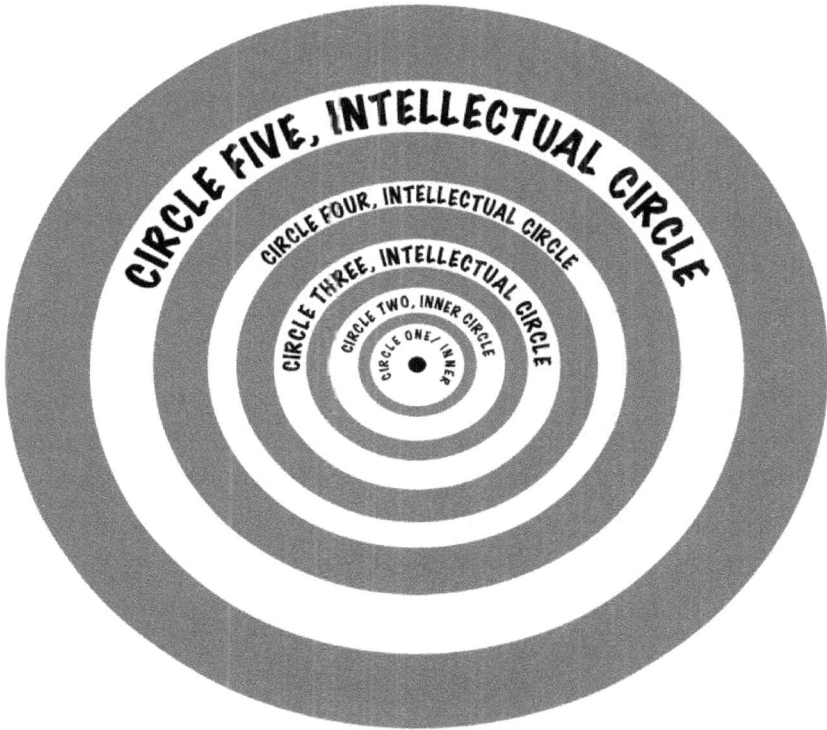

One of the most asked questions is—how do I transition a person out of my intimate circle into my intellectual circle? The answer is simple. You can lower yourself to speak with them from time to time, but don't make this a common practice, otherwise, you'll find yourself stuck. A realm can become a stronghold if you spend too much time in it. Think of it this way. Your friend lives 45 minutes away from you, and every time you two want to hang out, you are the one who has to travel to her. You have to gas up your vehicle and drive for 45 minutes to her because she doesn't have a car. However, if she was a good friend, she'd help you with the gas, right? But she's not doing that. Instead, she asks you to come and see her, and you do just that. In this situation, the proper thing to do would be to ask her for gas money from time to time because, in order for a relationship to be healthy, it has to be mutually beneficial. You can also request and require that she takes an Uber to see you sometimes, but let's be honest. The moment you put those stipulations on her, she'd go out of her way to make you feel bad, and the majority of her sentences would start off with, "You know my situation!" Let's say that you counter her words by reminding her that her situation has been the same for the last six years, and she isn't doing anything to change it. This means that, if allowed, she would continue to benefit from your relationship with her, while you continue to make sacrifices. Isn't this the very definition of idolatry? What am I saying here? When seasons change, a relationship that was once good and Godly can easily become demonic and one-sided. Now, am I saying that remaining friends with someone who refuses to grow is ungodly and demonic? Am I saying that remaining friends with someone who isn't as blessed as you are in any given season is a waste of time? Of course not! What I am saying is that every season requires a new level of sacrifice, and whenever you find yourself sacrificing more for a friend (or any person for that matter) than that individual is sacrificing for you season after season, you no longer have a friend. You have a mentee or a user on your hands. Remember, in order for any relationship to produce good fruits, you have to place the right label on it. If you don't set up the proper boundaries or use the right labels, you will find yourself in a different relational dynamic than the one you previously enjoyed with that friend. In other words, you may suddenly find yourself as the giver (Producer) while your friend or loved one serves as a taker (Consumer). There's nothing wrong with relationships shifting, whereas in one season, you're up and you're helping your friend, and the next season, you're down and your friend is helping you. Remember, this is called the Seesaw Effect, and it is the very heartbeat of relationships, but when the seesaw never shifts, whereas, you're always holding your friend or loved one up, while they are keeping you down, it is only a matter of time before you grow weary. All the same, please understand that humans cannot handle free stuff. What do I mean by this? If you repeatedly give something valuable to a person freely, what you're giving that person will lose its value to that person. In short, the taker will become, not only entitled, but he or she will discount or devalue the sacrifices you are making for him or her. For example, let's say that you are pretty skilled at styling hair, and while others pay you to style their hair, you never charge your big sister to style her hair. You'll notice that any time you say that you're too tired or you're not available to style her hair, she will respond negatively. If you ever put a boundary in front of her in the form of an invoice, she may curse at you, even if what you're charging her is 50 percent less than what you charge your clients for that same hairstyle. Rather than spending her money on you, she'll pay someone else one hundred percent of the fee, because she now feels entitled to your time, your hands, your products and your gifting. Unfortunately, this is the nature of the fallen man; this is just how the flesh responds to freebies. Simply put, most people can't handle being blessed. It brings out the worst in them. This means that if you repeatedly hold someone up, all the while allowing that person to keep you down, the individual in question will become accustomed to that particular dynamic. Consequently, the minute you complain about the situation, the person will respond with, "You know my situation!" This is why a lot of millionaires won't befriend people who are on different planes than themselves financially. Going back to the mountain example, let's say that Fred is at the top of the financial mountain with over five million dollars, but Frank is at the bottom of that same mountain with fifty dollars. Frank says to Fred, "Hey, let's go to dinner!" This is great; it's what friends do, but what Fred will come to discover is that he'll have to foot the bill 99 percent of the time. This is okay if Frank is on the path to financial freedom, but if Frank is in a stronghold, meaning he's not doing anything to grow financially, it would be unwise for Fred to entangle himself with Frank in the financial realm because he will be repeatedly taken advantage of by his friend.

The point is—our worldviews are determined by:
1. Where we stand.
2. Where we've stood (experience).
3. Where we're headed.
4. The conditions of our hearts.
5. What we know and understand.
6. The worlds that we're in.
7. The people we surround ourselves with (environment).

Let's talk about number three, which is "where we're headed." I want to make sure that you understand that where a person is headed isn't necessarily where that person is supposed to be. Every path that we take has different sights and experiences. Let's say that Donnie is supposed to be on the path towards financial freedom, but this path starts with him chasing God with all of his might and strength, and from there, he was supposed to create a Christian blog, go viral and ultimately find himself owning his very own podcast studio. This studio wouldn't just be the site of his ever-so-popular show; it would also have already setup rooms that other podcasters can rent. Nevertheless, Donnie is on another path, and he's been on that path for the last 17 years. Donnie has a radio show, but he's not talking about Christ or Christianity on his show. Instead, he's talking about motorcycles. Every path leads to a period. Think of it this way—every sentence or written thought is followed by a period. That period concludes that sentence, but it doesn't necessarily conclude the thought. You can continue talking about that particular subject for the entirety of that paragraph, article or book. This means that everything is subject-driven. So, while there's nothing wrong with Donnie having a show about motorcycles, it has led him and others to draw a conclusion about him, and that conclusion is—Donnie is "the Motorcycle Maniac." This is the nickname that his listeners have adjusted to. The conclusion is the period at the end of a sentence or season. It is what locks us into that season.

One day, Donnie is called to the front of the church by his

pastor. His pastor then begins to prophesy over him. He says to Donnie, "Right path, wrong mountain. This is what I keep hearing every time I look at you. You're supposed to be in ministry, Donnie, and I think you know this." Donnie lowers his head as he raises his hands. After the pastor is silent, Donnie responds with these words, "I know. My plate has just been so full these days. As soon as I can cut some time out of my schedule, I'm going to read my Bible more, start volunteering at the church and get into a few ministry classes." What is Donnie doing wrong? He's put his passion before his purpose, and this perversion of priorities could lead Donnie further and further into financial bondage. All the same, in order to fill your plate with God's plans, you must first empty it of your own plans. In conclusion, the way to transition out of an expired, toxic or ungodly relationship is to simply get on the right path. Remember Amos 3:3 says, "Can two walk together, except they be agreed?"

You're going to work next to people in parallel worlds, worship next to people in parallel worlds and live with people whose worlds are parallel to yours. The goal is to ensure that you are conscious and aware of, not just the world you're in but the world the people around you are in. This will help you to be less offended and more productive. How so? You won't put pressures or responsibilities on people who simply don't have the ability to carry those responsibilities out. All the same, you won't argue with people who are on the bottom of any given mountain that you stand atop of. You'll give them the revelation and the warnings that they'll need to ascend and protect themselves. If they take that information and allow it to illuminate their worlds al the more, great! You will have found someone to impart into. If they disregard that information, great! That is as long as it doesn't directly impact your life. I'll say it this way. As a mentor and a leader, I've been privileged to share what I've learned with many people; most people listen while others are combative. I don't complain or whine about the rebellious ones, after all, God has given us two teachers; they are Wisdom and Experience. Some people will sit in Wisdom's classroom and learn from her while others need the heavy hands of Experience to soften their hearts. Experience is Wisdom's belt carrier or disciplinarian; it is the alternative school for double-minded believers who keep looking for shortcuts to success (whatever success looks like to them). This is to say—don't be so easily hurt or offended whenever someone doesn't share the same worldviews or convictions as you do. Just make sure that you're on the right path, and all will be well.

Toxic Loyalty

In the previous Relational Acuity books, I briefly mentioned the concept of toxic loyalty. There is healthy loyalty, and then there is toxic loyalty. First, let's look at the definition of loyalty. Oxford Languages defines the word "loyalty" as "a strong feeling of support or allegiance." What if our parents were so committed to the third grade that they'd never left it? What if we had to sit in the same classrooms as them? What if they forbade us from graduating from that particular grade because they didn't want to be left behind? What would you do if those same parents had ceased communicating with over ninety percent of their family simply because their loved ones had dared to go past the third grade, and to add insult to injury, they'd gone all the way to the 12th grade before graduating? To them, the most insulting ones are the family members who dared to go to college! In the third grade, you would find yourself at a crossroads of sorts. You could honor your parents' unusual demand or you could make good grades. Of course, when you're eight-years old, you're immature and you care a lot about what your parents think and feel. So, you stay behind; that is until you're 14-years old. At this age, you notice that you're taller than most of your classmates and you have much more to talk about than they do. You could study hard so that you can be placed in the 7th or 8th grade, but doing this would put you at odds with your parents. If you decided to stay behind, you would be bound by toxic loyalty.

Toxic loyalty is usually built on one of six foundations:
- Fear.
- Tenure.
- Familiarity.
- Pity.
- Dependency.
- Transactionalism .

I'm not saying that these are the only foundations for toxic loyalty, but they are the main ones.

Fear

When toxic loyalty is built on the foundation of fear, it is generally centered around a belief that, for example, you can't live, function or prosper without the person you've linked yourself to. A great example of this is a woman who is married to a narcissistic and abusive man. When asked why she tolerates his abuse, she says, "I've been with him for seven years. He's all I know at this point, plus, he's the breadwinner. I don't think I could survive without him." Can she live without him? Absolutely, but whenever a person has been trapped in a season for quite some time, and they've never seen anything more productive than that particular season, that person will oftentimes fear change.

Tenure

When toxic loyalty is built on the foundation of tenure or time served, it is often centered around the belief that you owe a person your time, resources or a certain measure of favor in your life simply because that person has been a part of your life for an extended amount of time. It is great to be loyal to the people who are most dear and loyal to you, but it becomes toxic when those people are no longer serving your best interest or vice versa. A great example of this can be found in Matthew 20:1-16, which reads, "For the kingdom of heaven is like unto a man that is an householder, which went out early in the morning to hire laborers into his vineyard. And when he had agreed with the laborers for a penny a day, he sent them into his vineyard. And he went out about the third hour, and saw others standing idle in the marketplace, and said unto them; Go ye also into the vineyard, and whatsoever is right I will give you. And they went their way. Again he went out about the sixth and ninth hour, and did likewise. And about the eleventh hour he went out, and found others standing idle, and saith unto them, Why stand ye here all the day idle? They say unto him, Because no man hath hired us. He saith unto them, Go ye also into the vineyard; and whatsoever is right, that shall ye receive. So when even was come, the lord of the vineyard saith unto his steward, Call the laborers, and give them their hire, beginning from the last unto the first. And when they came that were hired about the eleventh hour, they received every man a penny. But when the first came, they supposed that they should have received more; and they likewise received every man a penny. And when they had received it, they murmured against the goodman of the house, saying, These last have wrought but one hour, and thou hast made them equal unto us, which have borne the burden and heat of the day. But he answered one of them, and said, Friend, I do thee no wrong: didst not thou agree with me for a penny? Take that thine is, and go thy way: I will give unto this last, even as unto thee. Is it not lawful for me to do what I will with mine own? Is thine eye evil, because I am good? So the last shall be first, and the first last: for many be called, but few chosen." In this example, we find the first responders feeling entitled to the greater portion simply because of their tenure. Nevertheless, a man who gets saved in the last moments of his life will enjoy the same Heaven and the same God that the man who accepted Jesus Christ as his Savior when he was seven-years old. All the same, we see this issue in businesses and churches alike.

Familiarity

When toxic loyalty is built on familiarity, it often centers itself around personal relationship dynamics. For example, a mother may feel entitled to her son's time and resources, even though her son is married. She may completely disrespect or disregard his wife altogether by asking or demanding things from her son, and then becoming offended if and when the son says, "Let me ask my wife first." Make no mistake about it—a relationship like this is incestuous in nature, even though the mother has never had an improper physical encounter with her son (hopefully). The mother may then respond by saying, "Why do you have to ask her?! I'm your mother! I carried you for nine months, spent 12 hours in labor with you, and I put a roof over your head, clothes on your back and food on the table!" In this, the mother is suggesting that her rank and position in the son's life should be greater than that of his wife. If the son does not set boundaries with his mother, he cannot and will not properly cleave to his wife. Consequently, he will become a victim of toxic loyalty. Relationships like these are often chaotic, and they tend to end in divorce. We also see this dynamic in every relational category, whereas one person will feel entitled to rank, power, favor and mercy simply because he or she is familiar with someone in rank. If the person in rank does not correct this behavior, his or her loyalty to that person will be rendered toxic or demonic. A great example of this can be found in the biblical account of Eli and his sons. Let's look at that story.

- **1 Samuel 2:12–17:** Now the sons of Eli were sons of Belial; they knew not the LORD. And the priests' custom with the people was, that, when any man offered sacrifice, the priest's servant came, while the flesh was in seething, with a fleshhook of three teeth in his hand; and he struck it into the pan, or kettle, or caldron, or pot; all that the fleshhook brought up the priest took for himself. So they did in Shiloh unto all the Israelites that came thither. Also before they burnt the fat, the priest's servant came, and said to the man that sacrificed, Give flesh to roast for the priest; for he will not have sodden flesh of thee, but raw. And if any man said unto him, Let them not fail to burn the fat presently, and then take as much as thy soul desireth; then he would answer him, Nay; but thou shalt give it me now: and if not, I will take it by force. Wherefore the sin of the young men was very great before the LORD: for men abhorred the offering of the LORD.
- **1 Samuel 2:22–25:** Now Eli was very old, and heard

all that his sons did unto all Israel; and how they lay with the women that assembled at the door of the tabernacle of the congregation. And he said unto them, Why do ye such things? For I hear of your evil dealings by all this people. Nay, my sons; for it is no good report that I hear: ye make the LORD'S people to transgress. If one man sin against another, the judge shall judge him: but if a man sin against the LORD, who shall intreat for him? Notwithstanding they hearkened not unto the voice of their father, because the LORD would slay them.

- **1 Samuel 2:27-36**: And there came a man of God unto Eli, and said unto him, Thus saith the LORD, Did I plainly appear unto the house of thy father, when they were in Egypt in Pharaoh's house? And did I choose him out of all the tribes of Israel to be my priest, to offer upon mine altar, to burn incense, to wear an ephod before me? And did I give unto the house of thy father all the offerings made by fire of the children of Israel? Wherefore kick ye at my sacrifice and at mine offering, which I have commanded in my habitation; and honourest thy sons above me, to make yourselves fat with the chiefest of all the offerings of Israel my people? Wherefore the LORD God of Israel saith, I said indeed that thy house, and the house of thy father, should walk before me for ever: but now the LORD saith, Be it far from me; for them that honour me I will honour, and they that despise me shall be lightly esteemed. Behold, the days come, that I will cut off thine arm, and the arm of thy father's house, that there shall not be an old man in thine house. And thou shalt see an enemy in my habitation, in all the wealth which God shall give Israel: and there shall not be an old man in thine house for ever. And the man of thine, whom I shall not cut off from mine altar, shall be to consume thine eyes, and to grieve thine heart: and all the increase of thine house shall die in the flower of their age. And this shall be a sign unto thee, that shall come upon thy two sons, on Hophni and Phinehas; in one day they shall die both of them. And I will raise me up a faithful priest, that shall do according to that which is in mine heart and in my mind: and I will build him a sure house; and he shall walk before mine anointed for ever. And it shall come to pass, that every one that is left in thine house shall come and crouch to him for a piece of silver and a morsel of bread, and shall say, Put me, I pray thee, into one of the priests' offices, that I may eat a piece of bread.

Because of familiarity, Eli exalted his sons above the priesthood; he prioritized their feelings over his responsibilities to God's people. Consequently, Eli found himself wrestling with toxic loyalty, and this stronghold or soul tie was so strong that he didn't bother repenting after the prophet addressed his behavior, nor did he repent when Samuel told him what the Lord said regarding him.

- **1 Samuel 3:10-19**: And the LORD came, and stood, and called as at other times, Samuel, Samuel. Then Samuel answered, Speak; for thy servant heareth.

21

And the LORD said to Samuel, Behold, I will do a thing in Israel, at which both the ears of every one that heareth it shall tingle. In that day I will perform against Eli all things which I have spoken concerning his house: when I begin, I will also make an end. For I have told him that I will judge his house for ever for the iniquity which he knoweth; because his sons made themselves vile, and he restrained them not. And therefore I have sworn unto the house of Eli, that the iniquity of Eli's house shall not be purged with sacrifice nor offering for ever. And Samuel lay until the morning, and opened the doors of the house of the LORD. And Samuel feared to shew Eli the vision. Then Eli called Samuel, and said, Samuel, my son. And he answered, Here am I. And he said, What is the thing that the LORD hath said unto thee? I pray thee hide it not from me: God do so to thee, and more also, if thou hide any thing from me of all the things that he said unto thee. And Samuel told him every whit, and hid nothing from him. And he said, It is the LORD: let him do what seemeth him good. And Samuel grew, and the LORD was with him, and did let none of his words fall to the ground. And all Israel from Dan even to Beersheba knew that Samuel was established to be a prophet of the LORD. And the LORD appeared again in Shiloh: for the LORD revealed himself to Samuel in Shiloh by the word of the LORD.

Pity

Believe it or not, this brand of toxic loyalty is more

common than you think, especially amongst women. Think back to the Seesaw Effect. In any good and healthy relationship, you will see movement. One season, you'll notice one friend pouring into and encouraging the other friend, and in the next season, the tables will turn. Howbeit, in a Consumer/Producer relationship, the Producer will remain at the bottom while attempting to hold the Consumer up. In this relational dynamic, there will be little to no movement, meaning the relationship is dead and the Producer is carrying around dead weight. If questioned, the Producer will oftentimes drop his or her head and say, "I feel sorry for him" or "I feel sorry for her." The Consumer will continue to pull on the Producer's heartstrings; that is until the Producer draws, establishes and enforces boundaries that prohibit the Consumer from taking advantage of the Producer any further. The woman may say to her lover, "Hey, at the beginning of next week, you will have to start taking the bus to work. I need my car." Then again, she may say to her sister, "Here, I'm serving you a thirty-day eviction notice. I'm giving you thirty days to find a job and get yourself a place. Starting February 1st, you will no longer be permitted to live in my house and sleep on my couch." This is when the Consumer will bear his or her fangs, but not before pulling on the Producer's heartstrings yet again. If this tactic doesn't work, the Consumer will often go out of his or her way to hurt or destroy the person who once helped him or her. Consider the parable that Jesus shared in Matthew 18:23–35, which states. "Therefore is the kingdom of heaven likened unto a certain king, which would take account of his servants. And when he had begun to reckon, one was brought unto him, which owed him ten thousand talents. But forasmuch as he had not to pay, his lord commanded him to be sold, and his wife, and children, and all that he had, and payment to be made. The servant therefore fell down, and worshipped him, saying, Lord, have patience with me, and I will pay thee all. Then the lord of that servant was moved with compassion, and loosed him, and forgave him the debt. But the same servant went out, and found one of his fellowservants, which owed him an hundred pence: and he laid hands on him, and took him by the throat, saying, Pay me that thou owest. And his fellowservant fell down at his feet, and besought him, saying, Have patience with me, and I will pay thee all. And he would not: but went and cast him into prison, till he should pay the debt. So when his fellowservants saw what was done, they were very sorry, and came and told unto their lord all that was done. Then his lord, after that he had called him, said unto him, O thou wicked servant, I forgave thee all that debt, because thou desiredst me: Shouldest not thou also have had compassion on thy fellowservant, even as I had pity on thee? And his lord was wroth, and delivered him to the tormentors, till he should pay all that was due unto him. So likewise shall my heavenly Father do also unto you, if ye from your hearts forgive not every one his brother their trespasses." Thankfully, the king in this story does not exemplify toxic loyalty; instead, he immediately addressed and corrected the unforgiving servant the moment he'd heard of his wicked deeds. However, he'd pitied the man, and this pity could have led him into the trap of toxic loyalty. In other words, the story could have ended differently. He could have allowed the man to remain free, while the man in question held another human in captivity. This would have affected his kingdom altogether because bystanders would have questioned his integrity, his discernment, his motives and his reason for allowing this man to practice hypocrisy. It would have also encouraged those under his kingdom to be both entitled and unforgiving. I can truly say that a lot of coaching and counseling calls that I've had were with women who were allowing men, friends or family members to take advantage of them, and they would always respond with, "I feel sorry for (insert freeloader's name here)."

Dependency

This toxic soul tie is the stuff that premeditated murders are made of! I said it once, and I'll say it again—people cannot handle unmerited favor (unless God preps and primes them for it)! They cannot repeatedly get freebies without it messing with the way that they think! Don't believe me? Put some strong boundaries around public assistance and watch what happens. Of course, there are people out there who need and deserve public assistance; this goes without saying, but we'd be lying to ourselves if we didn't acknowledge that a lot of the people who are receiving public assistance are taking advantage of and manipulating the system, after all, the love of money is the root of all evil. When someone repeatedly receives something that he or she did not work for, that person will start suffering from an addiction called dependency. Make no mistake about it; dependency is a drug. I know because I grew up in poverty and I've overheard more conversations about how to rob the system than I care to admit. I remember listening to a relative tell my mother how much money she could make if she'd gotten a mental evaluation for one of my siblings and had that sibling declared to be mentally ill. According to her, this was "free money." Dependency is the drug that keeps a lot of people in poverty from getting free. You see, in order to break out of the system, you have to undergo a season of inconvenience, and in this season, you have to face and address your fears, push through the obstacles and silence every no you've ever told yourself. Check out this story below:

> "The son of a rural Oklahoma newspaper publisher fatally shot his father, mother and sister, believing that by killing his family, he would inherit money to pay off mounting debts, a prosecutor said Wednesday.
> Prosecutors in Duncan filed three charges of first-degree murder against University of Oklahoma student Alan Hruby, 19, in the killings of his father, John, 50; mother, Tinker, 48; and his 17-year-old sister, Katherine, court records show. Alan Hruby did not yet have an attorney.
> Stephens County District Attorney Jason Hicks said Hruby owed money to a loan shark. Hicks did not say why Hruby had so much debt, only that his spending was out of control" (Source: CBS News/Prosecutor: Son killed Okla. family for inheritance).

What happened in this story? His dependency or addiction

was not just to money, but to the opinions of people. He was a rejected and entitled soul who desired to impress his peers. Check out this snippet from an article posted by Morbidology:

> "It soon became apparent that Alan was living much beyond his means and reveled in the notion that people found his wealth to be impressive. Well, his parents' wealth which he proclaimed to be his own wealth. According to students at the University of Oklahoma, Alan often bragged about how wealthy he was and would go on spending splurges. He wore a Rolex watch, Louis Vuitton shoes and flew first class. He often tagged his social media posts with "expensive" and mocked people who ate instant noodles. When he stole his grandmother's credit card, he took a trip to Europe and spent $5,000. Two years beforehand, he had assaulted his mother during an argument over money.
>
> Alan said that after the murders, he took the surveillance footage from the home recording system and fled to the University of Oklahoma in the jeep that his father had purchased him as a gift. He then went to a party at the Ritz-Carlton. According to Alan, he had been motivated to commit the murders because he had been cut off financially. His family said that he could not control his spending; he owed $3.000 to a Norman loan company and was being investigated for having stolen and forged $17,500 worth of checks. Alan stated that he believed if he killed his family, he would inherit their estate" (Source:

Morbidology.com/The Hruby Family Murders/Emily G. Thompson).

Sadly enough, two addictions had managed to form in his life, and his family had been unknowingly fueling one of those addictions. When they cut him off from his drug of choice, he decided to take their lives so that he could get unlimited access to his drug: money. This is the power of dependency. Believe it or not, dependency is not just limited to money. An abuser can become addicted to harming or hurting his lover or wife. Every time she returns to him or stays with him, she will unwittingly fuel his addiction, not just to abuse her but to have highly emotional moments of reconciliation. Understand this—when an abusive man or woman cries and begs his or her lover to stay, the abuser is not demonstrating a moment of humility, repentance or love. The abuser is having withdrawal symptoms; he or she may feel unloved in that moment and is looking for anything from a hug to an apology to makeup sex. Ask any person who's suffered at the hands of an abuser and he or she will tell you that the day of and, in many cases, a few days prior to the "punch," the abuser had been showing signs of depression and agitation. Why is this? These are withdrawal symptoms! The abuser wants to feel loved, but a hug, a bouquet of roses or a set of carefully crafted compliments won't do! The abuser gets his first drug from the adrenaline rush he experiences the moment he hits his lover; he gets his second drug the moment his lover comforts him. This is why relationships like those often end in murder. When the victim starts pulling away from the abuser, the abuser feels cut off from his or her drug. This can and often does lead to the abuser stalking the victim and ultimately taking that person's life. Again, this is not centered around love; it centers itself around addiction and dependency.

Transactionalism

Of course, this isn't a word that you'll find in your dictionary, but I'm using it to describe addictions formed as a result of transactional mindsets. What is a transactional mindset? It's when a person feels indebted to another person because of something that person did for him or her, or what that person represents to him or her. A lot of broken, immature and narcissistic men, for example, capitalize on this mindset by taking women out to eat, buying them gifts or taking them on trips. What this does to some women is it makes them feel indebted to those men. Consequently, they end up giving the guys sexual favors because they can't afford to "repay" them or because they have no ceiling over their concept of gratitude. What this means is that they magnify every small deed done for them; this is often because of rejection and unaddressed voids. They then attempt to balance out or repay the men they are now reverencing as heroes and good guys by offering their bodies to them. This is especially common in areas where there is widespread poverty. Understand this—we all have a measure of gratitude, and sometimes, we don't have anywhere to place the weight of our gratitude; this is especially true if we are surrounded by takers (Consumers). Because of this, we will often unload our gratitude on the first person who does a good deed for us, either great or small. In other words, we'll overcompensate for what we believe to be our shortcomings. Over the course of time, this can create a toxic soul tie between us and the people we feel indebted to. Ultimately, they may come into agreement with our belief that we should be repeatedly giving goods and favors to them, while they are not required to do anything for us. Again, this creates an addiction, as the human soul cannot handle unmerited favor when it becomes a constant in their lives. Notice throughout the Bible that those who had favor with God had their favor interrupted by seasons of testing and warfare.

Toxic loyalty is often secured by demonic and ungodly soul ties. As a reminder, the soul is comprised of the mind, will and emotions, and the mind, biblically speaking, is the heart. This is what God told us to guard. Therefore, when we soul tie ourselves to others in an ungodly way, we can easily find ourselves the victims of toxic loyalty, especially if we:

- Fail to set the proper boundaries.
- Fail to enforce our boundaries.
- Fail to address every repeated offense.
- Fail to employ disciplinary action against anyone who violates our boundaries.
- Allow the disrespect, abuse or dependency to interweave itself into the culture of our relationship.
- Fall into the trap of pitying someone who does not pity us.

- Confuse enabling someone with forgiveness.

If you want to have good and healthy relationships that are fueled by Godly loyalty, you have to:

1. Understand when a relationship is expired and when a season shifts, and then you have to respond accordingly.
2. Never remain at the bottom of the Seesaw Effect. If you notice that the person you're lifting up is rarely able to lift you up, you have to be okay with letting that person down. Enabling a person is not helping them; it's validating their entitlement.
3. Heal. Healed people are attracted to healed people. This doesn't mean that you should not help or build a relationship with broken and bruised souls; it means that you have to place the right labels on and boundaries around each relationship. This way, you don't end up becoming a replacement for God in anyone's life.
4. Set boundaries, enforce those boundaries and uphold those boundaries. By this, I mean don't lower your boundaries just because, for example, your mother stops calling you, your insignificant other breaks up with you or your friends abandon you. If this happens, it simply means that your boundaries are doing what they're supposed to do—keeping bound people at bay!
5. Get therapy and stop apologizing for escaping the seasons that your loved ones have become slaves to.
6. Build. Builders typically make great friends, confidants and potential spouses, but please

understand that builders are busy people! If you're accustomed to talking on the phone every single day for hours on end, building relationships with builders will serve as a culture shock to you because most builders don't like small talk. They share ideas, stories and useful info. This means that you'll have to busy up your time being productive.

7. Burn the bridge between your purpose and your comfort zone. This means that you have to take risks. Faith without risks is impotent. You do this by signing up for some classes and making commitments that lean into your purpose. You also do this by surrounding yourself with wise counselors and asking them to hold you accountable.

8. Practice taking accountability for your mistakes. People who have ascended or are ascending the mountains you're called to have learned that it's easier to ascend when you cast your burdens away from you. If you are always pointing the fingers of blame at others, you will be classified as a burden and people will cast you away from them.

9. Mature. You do this by having a strict Bible study schedule, never forsaking the coming together of the saints and applying what you've learned along the way. You also do this by surrounding yourself with wise counsel, purchasing books that can help you understand Kingdom principles all the more and by following some of today's most anointed and brilliant teachers.

10. Give. Yes, giving attracts predatory people, but it also brings you before great men (see Proverbs

18:16). The obvious question is—how do I protect myself from the predatory Consumers who will follow the trail of my good deeds? It's simple. You have to draw and enforce boundaries around your heart and your gifts.

If you were to speak with a large majority of my family, they would likely tell you that I'm in no way family-oriented. Some of them would frown before proudly proclaiming, "I ain't heard from her in years!" (Note: Most of us are from the Deep South). And, get this, they wouldn't be lying at all! I don't believe that I have to remain connected to people simply because we share the same DNA. I do, however, believe that my family will always hold a special place in my heart. The same is true for most people whose paths lead them away from their families. This means that our families have a measure of favor with many of us, but this favor should never encourage us to enable toxic behaviors, patterns or beliefs, nor should it encourage us to become a party to toxic loyalty. Instead, it should be used to help people who are trying to help themselves. In this, I immediately think about an aunt of mine (I mentioned this particular aunt in Relational Acuity 1.0). I hadn't heard from her in years. In truth, I hadn't heard from her since I was a little girl, even though she lived in town. I had been taught that family members like her thought they were better than us, but I won't go too far into that silly belief. I remember when I briefly reconnected with her. I was excited about finally building a relationship with this elusive aunt. I remembered how fond I had been of her when I was a kid and how confused I was when she'd stopped coming around, and that's when I'd been introduced to the concept that she thought she was better than the rest of us. Why? Because she was successful, and on top of being successful, she'd stopped sounding like us. She didn't use broken English (Ebonics and Southern slang) and she didn't seem to subscribe to what we regarded as Black culture anymore. What I didn't realize at the time was that every world has a language and every dimension of that world has a dialect. To enter into any given industry or world, you have to learn the language of that particular world. You can't enter into a new world exalting the language of your former world, otherwise, if this behavior is tolerated, you'll create a split in that world, whereas some people will come to you to complain about the principles and principalities of that world, and the rulers of that particular world (principalities) will feel the need to defend their beliefs and their world altogether. So, to prevent this split from happening, any world that you dishonor will ultimately spit you out of it. This is why Jesus, when referencing double-minded believers, said in Revelation 3:16, "So, because you are lukewarm, and neither hot nor cold, I will spit you out of my mouth." Remember, a world isn't always a planet; it is a system. We are in Christ; this means that we are a part of the system that transforms us by the renewing of our minds, and then translates us into the Kingdom of God. I mentioned this particular aunt because I remember something she said to me. She warned me about some of our family members. After telling me that she saw something special in me, she told me in plain Southern English, "Don't let them get over on you!" Howbeit, this wasn't the most significant thing she'd said that day. What I remember most is the fact that she was financially supporting one of my cousins who was in college. "I help her because she's trying to help herself," she said. In this, she introduced me to the principle that you should never help someone who doesn't value or believe in themselves enough to help themselves, otherwise, you'll literally be casting your pearls to reckless people (swine).

My time with that particular aunt was short-lived because she'd stopped communicating with me when she realized that I was not interested in converting to her religion, but I believe that God allowed me to get the impartation I needed before closing that door between us. Like many African Americans, I've been raised under the belief that "blood is thicker than water," and this particular aunt was living outside of that principle. This belief suggests that family is more important than any and everyone else, therefore, their opinions, desires and plans should take precedence over the opinions, desires and plans of anyone who is not related to us; this includes our spouses. Again, this is toxic loyalty. This belief isn't just limited to the South or to the African American community, it is also found in White America and in many cultures. All the same, it is a toxic belief that has to be unlearned as it is responsible for the destruction of many marriages, the splitting of many families and the mental depravity that some people suffer with. It allows jealousy, competition and the crab mentality to go unchecked, and it turns a blind eye to the abuse and mistreatment that many people suffer at the hands of their families. This is why I'm not super family-oriented. I'd spent my entire childhood being molested, defending myself and being submerged in a toxic family culture. Consequently, I started dealing heavily with lust at a very young age. It seemed that everyone was "bumping clothes" or "dry humping," meaning grinding with their clothes on. In other words, this behavior became normalized in my family. What was Satan doing? He was acclimating me to the belief that my body didn't belong to me. He was training me to be a seductress and an adulteress. I don't remember when the lights came on in my head, but once they did, I became increasingly avoidant of certain family members. That's when I realized just how dysfunctional my family was, especially when they gathered together. During the day, the adults would be drinking, arguing, gossiping or talking about matters that didn't pertain to them, but during the night, somebody would be having sex with or grinding on somebody. And this dysfunctional behavior is often swept under the rug, and the people who have found themselves in this type of family dynamic often deal heavily with guilt and shame. Many of them never tell their stories out of fear of being ridiculed, devalued or judged, or out of fear of implicating themselves. During one of our mentorship meetings, I allowed my students to open up about their childhood traumas, and it was surprising to me to hear the number of women who'd grown up in families like my own. Many of them had never told their stories before, so they cried as they talked about the things that had not only happened to them when they were younger, but what they had (initially) become as a result of those traumas. No one likes to admit that they've been involved in incest or pedophilia, even if they'd only engaged in those behaviors when they were children. Nevertheless, it is the will of God that we, along with our families, be set free. This is why I don't always encourage people to stay connected or reconnect with their families. I encourage them to heal, forgive and to move forward. If their families move forward with them, great! If their families stay behind, they cannot allow toxic loyalty to make them feel guilty for moving forward. If their families move against them, push against the pressure with the Word! Either way, we have to move forward. And again, family will always have a place in our hearts. With that said, I also encourage them to help those who want to break free, but never partner with any of the toxic and ungodly principles they were taught growing up.

I shared all of this because a lot of ungodly and toxic thought patterns and beliefs were taught to us when we were young, and get this—some of our families are knitted together by the threads of these beliefs. This means that by going against what you've been taught, you are also going against the grain of what holds your family together, and you have to be okay with this if you want to see them get saved, set free and healed. This is what I mean when I say I'm not family-oriented. In short, I am not a slave to the beliefs that held my family together outwardly while ripping us apart inwardly. I won't turn a blind eye to the devil, all the while pretending that he's not there. Instead, I went and got my freedom so that I could help as many people get free as possible, including family members.

Unlearning toxic beliefs is a pretty lonely journey,

especially in the beginning. Let's say that you've come from a highly dysfunctional family. You have to understand that you have a measure of dysfunction and toxicity because of the environment you've been in. Because of this, healthy, functional people won't necessarily invite you into their lives because they don't want you to disturb the peace in their lives. This means that you'll be caught between two seasons. Remember, the hallway between two seasons is the wilderness. This is when God addresses your traumas, your voids, your generational curses and everything that's been holding you back. When you're in this space, your assignment is to grieve, grow, heal and mature, and you do that by:

1. Studying the Word of God daily.
2. Planting yourself in a good, Bible-based church.
3. Surrounding yourself with a multitude of counselors.
4. Getting therapy.
5. Buying and reading books that will help you to heal, grow and further understand God's Word.
6. Confronting every lie and twisted truth that you've come to believe with the Word of God.
7. Giving yourself permission to offend any and everyone who sees your journey as a threat to their position in your life.

I got free because I questioned what I didn't understand, conducted my own research, took accountability, got therapy and forgave the hurt people who once hurt me. All the same, I didn't allow any of my loved ones or peers to bully me into accepting their truths as my own. They have their own relationships with God just like I have my own relationship with Him. What God taught me over time was that my relationship with Him should not look like another person's relationship with Him. Our relationship creates its own unique fingerprint, and this fingerprint forms our authenticity. It is my authenticity that gives me access to the blessings and the favor of God. I say that to say this—if you allow people to conform you to their worlds, you will be simultaneously relinquishing your authenticity, which means that you'll also be rejecting your God-given authority. And to seal your relationship with these people, you'll be encouraged to participate in toxic loyalty, also known as relational idolatry.

SOUL TIE SNATCHERS

The following snippet was taken from Biography.com:

> "In Salt Lake City in 2002, while she slept in the
> bedroom that she shared with her sister, 14-year-
> old Elizabeth Smart was kidnapped at knifepoint.
> She was dragged into the Utah woods and held
> prisoner by Brian David Mitchell, who referred to
> himself as Immanuel, and his wife, Wanda Barzee.
> Mitchell starved the girl, force-fed her drugs and
> alcohol, and raped her daily in an attempt to
> brainwash her into believing that he was a prophet.
> Mitchell and Barzee roamed Utah and California for
> almost nine months with Smart in tow before they
> were discovered and arrested" (Source:
> Biography.com/6 Famous Abductions and Where the
> Women Are Today/Joe McGasko).

Elizabeth Smart was only fourteen years old when her
kidnapper, Brian David Mitchell, snatched her. He saw a
young woman that he wanted and decided that her will or
ability to make a decision was subject to his own. In other
words, he robbed Ms. Smart of her ability to make a
decision and, of course, at the age of 14, her parents were
her legal guardians, meaning she wasn't old enough to
make decisions about marriage and all that came with it.
However, Mr. Mitchell was a controller. Controllers or soul
tie snatchers don't care about what you think or how you
feel; they always embody the nature of Satan. God gave us

free will or the freedom of will; this is the ability to weigh out a matter and make our own decisions and, of course, our decisions come with rewards and penalties (consequences). Satan, on the other hand, desires to control people; we see the evidence of this in Genesis 6:1-5, which reads, "And it came to pass, when men began to multiply on the face of the earth, and daughters were born unto them, That the sons of God saw the daughters of men that they were fair; and they took them wives of all which they chose. And the LORD said, My spirit shall not always strive with man, for that he also is flesh: yet his days shall be an hundred and twenty years. There were giants in the earth in those days; and also after that, when the sons of God came in unto the daughters of men, and they bare children to them, the same became mighty men which were of old, men of renown. And GOD saw that the wickedness of man was great in the earth, and that every imagination of the thoughts of his heart was only evil continually." When the Bible talks about the sons of God in the Old Testament, the author is referencing angels, both good and fallen. When the Bible refers to the sons and daughters of mankind, the author is referencing humans. Therefore, this passage of scripture is talking about demonic spirits lying down with and marrying themselves to human beings. Notice that the author says "they took them wives of all which they chose." This means that they completely violated the wills of these women. Today, we still see human beings doing this. Extreme cases include kidnapping, sex-trafficking and blatantly holding someone against their will. Mild or normalized cases include seducing, lying and manipulating people into forming soul ties, and hear me when I say this—there are some people on this planet who are masterful at forming soul ties with others. This is especially true for narcissists; narcissistic men and women are often very skilled soul-tie snatchers.

What is a soul-tie snatcher? This is a person who quickly, strategically and sometimes forcefully creates soul ties with others. These indiv duals typically wrestle with fantasy. For example, they will fantasize about how a relationship with you can benefit them, and from there, they will go out of their way to establish a relationship with you, but they won't go about it the natural and Godly way. They will often use the following to establish soul ties with others:

1. Flattery.
2. Gift-giving.
3. Gossip/Slander.
4. Sex or Sexual Favors.
5. Their Power and Positions.
6. Victimhood (Pity).
7. Fear.
8. Offense.
9. Love-bombing.
10. Enticement (Sensuality, Empty Promises, Seduction).

Of course, this is just a short list of methodologies that soul-snatchers use to create soul ties. Why are people so determined to form quick soul ties with others? Because a lot of people are operating in survivor's mode, meaning they have not gotten past many of the traumas they've experienced. Because cf this, they go about looking for people who will love them, understand them and accept them as they are. Whenever they come in contact with people who they feel can be of some benefit to them, they quickly begin what I refer to as the soul tie ceremony. This three-day event is usually comprised of a series of phone calls, a whole lot of love-bombing, future-faking and planning an outing or two. People excitedly show up, for example, to the outing with the light of hope gleaming in their eyes. Finally, they've found someone who understands them! They breathe a subtle sigh of relief and tell their new friends or new lovers about all the hell they've gone through as they navigated the friendship space or the dating pool. The other party mirrors what they're saying and the date goes better than good! Howbeit, we don't have to continue this story to see how it ends. A soul tie forms, the people walk together for years and the relationships end on a bad note. Why is this? The short answer is—people keep trying to link their souls to people rather than allowing God to heal their souls. The long answer is—people try to use other people as void-fillers and bandages, rather than allowing God to fill those voids, heal their traumas and bring them into a place of contentment. Do you know who gets the worst of this? Leaders! This is because people see leaders as the solutions to their problems, and while a leader is a solutionist, the leader himself or herself is not the solution.

When I talk about leaders, I'm not just talking about pastors; I'm also talking about influencers. Most influencers can attest to the fact that they've lost followers simply because they wouldn't "sell their souls" to people. We've heard the concept of selling one's soul before, and when most people hear this phrase, they think about a person selling his or her soul to the devil; they think that it means that the person has volunteered to go to hell in exchange for fame and fortune on Earth or for a chance at revenge. Either way, we know that it is possible for a person to exchange his or her eternity for a moment here on Earth. All the same, Jesus asked a really thought-provoking question in Mark 3:36. He asked, "For what shall it profit a man, if he shall gain the whole world, and lose his own soul?" Let's keep in mind that the soul is comprised of the mind, will and emotions. Why is this important? Losing one's soul is not just something that takes place in the after-life; to lose your soul also means to lose the health of your mind here on Earth. This is why Proverbs 10:22 says, "The blessing of the LORD, it maketh rich, and he addeth no sorrow with it." This principle helps us to distinguish whether a blessing came from God or from the enemy. When God blesses us, He adds no sorrow to it, but when hell gifts us with something, it is filled with sorrow, regret and chaos. This is why it is foolish to chase riches. Some people attain the wealth and the lifestyles that they want, but they lose their minds, their marriages, their children and their credibility in the process. Listen, there is no amount of money, revenge or fame that is worth your peace! It is pointless to attain a lifestyle that you are not mentally healthy enough to enjoy; think about it. With that said, let me tell you about a dilemma that most leaders have to navigate their way through. Please try not to see it from the perspective of someone sitting in the audience. I want you to envision yourself as one of these leaders; this is how empathy is grown and your relational acuity is heightened. This is what we refer to as empathy.

First, let me share a testimony of my own. One of my sisters in Christ (let's call her Brenda) reached out to me one day to tell me about one of her friends (let's call her Deborah). Brenda and I are similar in many ways; this is why she elected me to be her mentor some years ago, and the relationship has since blossomed into a strong sisterhood. Sure, she's a friend of mine, but we focus more on our sisterhood than anything. This is because Brenda is still somewhat of a babe in Christ or, better yet, I'd say she's a teen in Christ, so our relationship still has those mentorship undertones, along with some big sister/little sister vibes. In short, we are always laughing at one another or fussing, and in most cases, I find myself helping Brenda get the language for the seasons she finds herself in. So, it comes as no shock to me when Brenda sends one of her friends my way for counseling. This is why she referred Deborah to me.

Deborah was in the middle of a storm and needed some wise counsel. After trying to help Deborah navigate the space she was in, Brenda told her about me and urged her to go to my website and book a coaching session with me. Brenda called me to tell me about Deborah's situation, citing that Deborah would be reaching out to me shortly. I thanked her for the reference and we went on to talk about other things. Deborah started texting me and I answered her messages before urging her to book a session with me. She did. When we were on the line together, she told me about her situation and, of course, I started advising and coaching her. Howbeit, Deborah did something that I absolutely despise. She kept trying to spin me around (see Relational Acuity 4.0) to speak with another side of me. This is what I call soul-tie snatching. To briefly explain this—we are multidimensional creatures, and we often present the face that people need or want access to, and by face, I'm not saying that we are being pretentious. I'm saying that we are all multifaceted creatures, meaning there are many sides to us. You have a financial face, just as you have a platonic face. You also have a familial face, a career or professional face and you have a religious face. Not everyone sees every side of you. For example, Toni may walk up to you at church, and when you see her coming, you'll spin around and show her your comedic face; this is because your comedic side is the only side of you that she can relate to or it's the only side of you that she is mature enough to see. Then again, it may be the only side of you that she pulls on. Notice I said pull and not snatch. The difference is that people who pull on you won't put unnecessary pressure on you, but soul-snatchers have already made it up in their minds which side of you that they want access to, and they never tell themselves that you may deny them access. This is why they are often caught off guard by the word "no." In the distance, you may see Margaret heading your way. Margaret has never seen your comedic side. Anytime you're around her, you show her your serious God-face; this is your sacred side. Are you being fake with either woman? No, not at all! You are simply giving each woman the side of you that they pull on the most. So, when

Margaret comes over to hug you, you may find yourself behaving maturely around her, all the while spinning around and acting silly with Toni. Toni then shouts out, "Ms. Margaret, can you rebuke her because she called me a pufferfish?" In this, Margaret may laugh and say, "No, she wouldn't say anything like that," before continuing to wherever she was headed. What happened here? In that moment, you had to navigate two relationships by giving each woman the face that she could relate to or the face she wanted to see, and because both Toni and Margaret stood next to you at the same time, both women saw another side of you. This is also why some people keep their friend groups separate. One friend group sees a side of them that the other friend group has never met, but people who have a high degree of relational and social intelligence can easily merge both or all of their friend groups. They can navigate each relationship in a single space without fear of negatively impacting other relationships.

Of course, you shouldn't always give people the face that they want, especially if you're a leader. You have to give them the side of you that they are mature enough to host. Therefore, when people pull on another side of you, you have to stonewall them. Please note that Oxford Languages defines the word "stonewall" as "delay or block (a request, process, or person) by refusing to answer questions or by giving evasive replies, especially in politics." What does stonewalling look like? Let's say that Toni is too immature to deal with financially, but yet and still, she tries to spin that side of you around. She asks,

"How much money do you make on your job?" Depending on the context by which the question was asked, this question could be construed as inappropriate, and if it is, you'd stonewall Toni in that area. How so? You'd give her a brief and evasive answer before spinning back around to show her the facet of you that you've granted her access to. This may sound like you jokingly saying, "Mind the business that pays you," before spinning back around and saying, "Did you see Tyler Perry's new movie? I laughed all the way through it!" In that moment, Toni may feel somewhat rejected, but get this, you didn't reject her. You simply denied her access to another side of you. Why is this? She may be too immature or too broken to access that side of you. At the same time, you may have reserved that type of information for people who are in your intimate circle; this is why it is important to pre-determine what allowances and limitations each circle of people in your life has. Then again, Margaret may try to joke with you one day; she may say, "When you wear your hair like that, you look like a pretzel." While this may have been funny if Toni said it, the problem is, you've never seen that particular side of Margaret, so you won't laugh as hard. Instead, you may find yourself giggling, all the while maintaining eye contact with Margaret to see if she's joking. This means that Margaret is pulling on your comedic side, and you may not necessarily want to give her access to that side of you because you take her seriously. To you, she's mature, well-rounded and sophisticated. Chances are, you'd make that moment so awkward that Margaret would never try to spin that side of you around again. She'd walk away from that moment wondering if she'd offended you, and she'd likely stop you later that day to apologize. "I didn't mean anything by it," she'd say. "I was just joking around." The point is—we are multifaceted, multidimensional people, but not everyone has access to every side of us. So, when I said that Deborah was trying to spin me around, I mean that she wanted access to the side of me that Brenda had access to. She kept trying to get too personal with me, and by this, I mean that she was trying to pry into my life. This was a counseling session; I had no intention of going outside of being Deborah's coach in that moment, after all, I didn't know her. Like most leaders, I find this highly annoying because it almost always leads to the person feeling rejected by us when this is not the case. Consequently, the individual walks away hurt, offended and, in some cases, feeling vengeful, and we walk away feeling robbed of our ability to make a choice in the matter. Howbeit, the call between Deborah and I went great, or so I thought. I advised her, she talked about setting up more sessions with me and all appeared to be well. A week or so later, Brenda told me that Deborah felt somewhat rejected by me (these weren't her exact words). She said that I had a wall up. Brenda went on to explain to her that I don't allow people into my life easily; when I set up a coaching session with someone, I'm going to stay in that particular vein. She further explained that I'm a great sister in Christ and friend, but I'm not always open to new relationships. When Brenda told me about their dialogue, she didn't tell me to incite a negative response; she wasn't trying to pit Deborah and I against one another. She was an advocate for the both of us, and no, she was not fussing at me for having that wall up. She was simply telling me how Deborah felt and how she'd responded. She also found it funny because I'd complained in the past about people setting up coaching sessions with me or joining my mentorship program, and then getting angry when I'd stonewalled them after they'd tried to access my platonic side. I wasn't mean to them; I simply gave them what I was offering (advice and mentorship), but I refused them access into my personal life.

Most leaders have a myriad of experiences that they can readily share, some of which they'll laugh about and some of which they'll cry about. Remember two things that we discussed: survivor's mode and voids. When these two come together, they not only create the whirlwinds of attraction, they create a force called control. You see, broken people tend to wrestle with either covert control or overt control, meaning they'll knowingly or unwittingly rob others of their abilities to make decisions. We witness it all the time. Every year, you'll find a lot of people leaving the traditional church scene, and not all of them were mishandled by church folks or leaders. Many of them went into the church with unrealistic expectations, and when those expectations were not met, they left the church feeling robbed and offended. Every relationship they've ever built was fast, emotionally intense and filled with love-bombing, gaslighting and witchcraft. In other words, a great deal of people come into the church not knowing how to form or have healthy, Godly relationships. Most churches don't have classes to teach people how to do this, and even if they did, I'm sure that most folks wouldn't see the need to register for those classes. This is because people have a tendency to focus on their intentions and not the conditions of their hearts. Remember, there is a speed limit to healthy relationships, but when a person has spent his or her entire life running past that speed limit, it's hard to get the person to slow down, be patient and allow any relationships that will form to grow organically. I've found that a lot of people are accustomed to selling pieces and portions of their souls to people, and they think that those people owe them access to their souls as well. This is a form of prostitution, and it is prevalent in the American church today, and not just with people attempting to soul tie themselves to leaders. It is also common with people trying to soul tie themselves to any and every person they feel can enhance their lives. When people consider building relationships with others, they consider the benefits and the drawbacks. If a person determines that building a relationship with you will be incredibly beneficial to him or her in any way, that person may go out of his or her way to establish that relationship, and this is fine if the relationship is going to be mutually beneficial and if the person doesn't try to rob you of your ability to choose whether or not you want to be in a relationship with him or her. Let's face it; most people want relationships that are beneficial to them, but they don't want the responsibilities associated with being a blessing in return. We all know this, even though most folks aren't willing to admit it. All the same, the individual has to be healthy enough to host the relationships that he or she wants. Lastly, we can't rob people of their abilities to make decisions regarding us; in other words, we can't force people to let us in their lives or friendship circles, nor should we ridicule, humiliate or punish them should they decide that they don't want to be our friends. In short, we have to stop trying to turn people into prostitutes, selling their souls in exchange for us not being mad at them. Think about it this way. If you're a woman, you've likely had a man to call you names or attempt to humiliate you simply because you turned down his advances. Was this fair to you? Are you obligated to give some dude your number just because he's interested in you? Of course, not! We understand this concept in situations like these, but when it comes to the church or Christians altogether, the rules seem to go out the window for most folks. I can't tell you how many times I've coached or counseled someone who was hurt or angry because they felt rejected by another human being. "I just wanted to be her friend," they said, focusing on their good intentions, and not realizing that the narcissists they once entertained in their own personal lives gave them a toxic trait. That toxic trait is soul-tie snatching and it looks like this:

1. Love-bombing another person.
2. Speeding in a relationship, thus forming quick soul ties.
3. Labeling people before they know them, for example, "I know we don't know each other well, but I feel like you're my best friend!"
4. Growing familiar with those people.
5. Equalizing every person in their lives.
6. Learning about the people and then gossiping about them. This typically comes from disappointment. In short, when people speed through relationships,

they often have great and grand expectations of the corresponding party, and when these expectations are not met, disappointment is inevitable. This disappointment is followed by offense, and this offense can and often leads to gossip, slander or ranting.

7. Discarding those people once they are of little to no benefit. Please note that discarding a person doesn't always look like you ending your relationship with that person. Some people discard other people by avoiding their calls, not returning their calls and ghosting them altogether. They resurface when they want something from the other person.

Challenge yourself to evaluate how you form relationships and how fast you give or accept intimate titles in those relationships. This is important if you want to establish good, Godly and healthy relationships with other people. Healthy relationships aren't rushed; they form over time, and they form organically. Whenever a person is trying to rush or force their way into your life, please understand that the person in question doesn't have a healthy soul. I immediately think about a guy Brenda introduced me to. At the time, she'd been renting the upstairs portion of her house to an Airbnb client, and after talking with the guy, she was convinced that she'd met my future husband. She was so convinced that she came to church on a Wednesday, and that was something Brenda just did not do. She came to church because she wanted me to see the picture of the guy and gauge my reaction. Church had already started when Brenda walked in, and I was on post, sitting near the VIP doors. As Brenda passed by me, she handed me her phone. She already had the guy's picture pulled up. She went to her seat, leaving me holding her phone and looking at the guy's photo. I didn't look very long. As she was taking her seat, I was getting out of mine. I walked up to Brenda, tapped her on the shoulder and handed her back her phone. She looked at me to see my reaction, but it wasn't the reaction she'd expected. I shook my head from side to side, indicating that my answer was no. I giggled when I saw the frown on Brenda's face. We had to keep quiet because my pastor was preaching, so Brenda lifted her index finger as if to say, "Wait one minute." When service was over, Brenda made her way to me. I laughed as I saw her approaching me with her trademark frown. "I sped through traffic to get here," she joked. "What's wrong with this one?!" I couldn't explain it; there was just something off about the guy and I didn't want to entertain him. After we fussed a little about the guy, I agreed to speak with him over the phone at least one time, after all, he wanted to publish his book through my company. Brenda excitedly left church, and later that night, the guy called me (we'll call him Tom). I'd spoken with Tom for a little over an hour when I'd said to him, "You're not my husband and I'm not your wife." I then began the benedictory process, hoping that we could still do business together without any attempts to get to know one another personally. I am completely aware of the fact that telling a strange man, "You are not my husband" is weird and maybe even uncalled for, but I learned a long time ago to let people know what you are thinking or what you've decided the moment you decide it; this way you don't lead them on. If you read Relational Acuity 4.0, you are aware of the cable guy story; I wanted to protect myself from anything like that ever happening again. What made me come to the conclusion that Tom wasn't the guy for me? In short, he was against the church, not for it. His book was written from a place of offense; he wanted to dismantle the church and, of course, he didn't have a church home or a pastor. He was just a man who'd gone to church, gotten offended and decided that every church in America needed to close its doors. In short, he was generalizing every church based on his experiences with one church, and Tom didn't want to listen to sound reasoning. His mind was made up, his book had been written, and now, all I had to do was get on board. As today's generation says so eloquently, I wasn't going. Yes, I did try to minister to him. I tried to help him understand what he'd gone through and I tried to point him to someone I believed could help him. Tom didn't want help; he wanted a publisher and a wife. That's it and that's all. All the same, Tom had romantic trauma that he hadn't gotten past. Of course, Brenda didn't initially know what I'd learned that night. He'd told her that he was Christian, he'd written a book and he was a graphic designer. I'm Christian, I've written several books and I'm a graphic designer, so Brenda thought she'd met her future brother-in-law.

"What do you mean I'm not your husband?" Tom countered. "I don't even know you and you don't know me!" Tom was clearly a refined man; he sounded sophisticated and somewhat uptight. In my mind, I was doing us both a favor. I didn't want Tom to assume that we were getting to know one another for the sake of potentially dating, courting and then marriage. We would definitely be unequally yoked, and I knew what the Bible says about that. I tried to keep my voice as ladylike and comforting as possible. "I understand," I said. "Brenda introduced you to me because she thought we'd make a great couple and she knew you were looking for a publisher. I'm simply acknowledging that I'm not the girl for you because I respect you enough to not waste your time. I respect myself enough to not waste my time as well." Tom wouldn't hear of it. He kept repeating, "How could you say something like that?! I don't know you and you don't know me!" I tried to change the tone and explain to him that we could be "cool," meaning I didn't mind talking with him every now and again. I was simply saying that we couldn't build anything outside of that. What I've learned about broken and toxic people is this—when you don't "beat around the bush" or play mind games with them, they'll start saying things that do not make sense. Tom was no different. On one hand, he kept reminding me that we didn't know each other and that he was okay with us not getting to know one another romantically, but on the other hand, he would not stop talking about me rejecting him romantically. "That's water under the bridge," I said. "Like I told you, we can be friends. Like you said, you weren't thinking about a romantic relationship, so what's the big deal?" Day after day, Tom would call me and he'd start fussing about what I'd said to him. "I just can't get over the fact that you said that I wasn't your husband and you're not my wife! You don't even know me." About three days into him calling me, I had no choice but to tell him to stop calling me, after all, we were just on the phone arguing about my decision, and not just my decision, but the realization I had regarding "us." There could be no "us" with Tom and I. Tom would go on to ignore every boundary I placed in front of him, including the one where I'd asked him not to call me after 10pm. Finally, I blocked Tom's phone number and I blocked him on social media. He was not a nice guy. He was definitely forceful, and I wouldn't have seen this side of him in so early if I'd just gone with the flow. Nevertheless, I'm older and wiser now, plus I truly respect the time of people. I hate when people waste my time, so I try not to waste the time of others. Tom would go on to make life difficult for Brenda. His demons couldn't hide themselves anymore, so while living in her Airbnb, Tom started making Brenda's house uncomfortable. She said he started flirting heavily with her, frequenting her kitchen and offering to cook her something to eat. He even started talking to her daughters, and this made her increasingly uncomfortable. After he kept violating her boundaries, Brenda ended her contract with him by simply not allowing him to renew the contract. Startled, she vowed to never allow another man to live in her Airbnb.

What were some of the red flags I saw with Tom?
1. I had an uncomfortable feeling when I looked at his picture.
2. He was bitter against the church.
3. He had no church home, no pastor and no one to hold himself accountable to.

4. Once I communicated my decision to him, he would not respect it. Tom was clearly one of those guys who didn't like women. I'm not saying that he was or is gay; I'm saying that while he wanted a wife, he didn't necessarily like women. This disdain for women manifested itself as his inability to respect the choice of a woman.

5. He kept violating my boundaries. Remember, bound people hate boundaries.

6. He wouldn't move forward in conversation; he kept reminding me of what I'd said in his attempt to force me into doing what he wanted. You see, this man hadn't seen me in person, so he couldn't say that he liked or loved me, but what triggered him was the fact that I'd taken his ability to control the narrative away from him by making a decision of my own. It was obvious that he kept trying to regain control. Without the ability to control me or the narrative, he felt like a fish out of water.

7. He kept trying to confuse me. I wanted to end the conversation about "us" and just talk about other things, but he kept trying to twist my words and make me feel guilty, confused and offended.

8. He was argumentative. I don't remember ever having a conversation with him that ended civilly.

9. He clearly wrestled with unforgiveness. This made it hard for him to hear what I was saying (present tense) because he kept hearing what I said (past tense).

10. Even though he'd claimed that he wasn't thinking about a relationship at that time, Tom could not

stop talking about his ex and how she'd betrayed him. Some people use repeated talks of their exes to prepare you to be their next.

Was Tom a bad guy? I don't know. What I do know is this—his convictions did not align with my own, and when I'd expressed this to him, he'd started gaslighting me. What would have been a better response? A healthy person would have acknowledged my decision, communicated his position with me, respected me as a person, honored my decision and moved on with his life. If we'd decided to talk every now and again, he would have allowed a friendship to blossom and see what would potentially come of that. A toxic person or a narcissist, on the other hand, doesn't like to be told no. They often wrestle with high-level rejection and take everything personally.

What if you are guilty of trying to formulate relationships with people, and then feeling rejected and offended whenever they keep showing you their professional face or their church face? How do you get past those not-so-pleasant feelings that emerge whenever you feel rejected?

1. Remind yourself that people aren't necessarily rejecting you. Sometimes, they've reached their friendship capacity. At other times, you may be pulling on a side of them that's under renovation. They may not like the speed limit you're going. They could be afraid of new relationships or they may be afraid of forming a new relationship with you because of your past, who you hang around, the way you throw yourself at them, and the list goes on.

2. Remind yourself that the will of another human is so sacred that even God, Himself, won't rob them of it. Trying to control the will of another human being is a form of witchcraft.

3. Get therapy. You may be in a space where you're looking for people to fill a void in your life, and you have to learn to navigate the season you're in with the people God has given you access to.

4. Cast down evil imaginations. It shocks and saddens me when I consider the fact that most people don't bother managing their minds, meaning they don't guard their hearts, they don't cast down evil imaginations and they never question their thoughts. Instead, they challenge and question others.

5. Go through deliverance if needed. Sometimes, a strong desire to connect to another person is completely demonic. Demons can and do riddle the minds of their hosts; this is why there have been cases, for example, of men seeing women from afar, and then telling themselves that those women are the right ones for them. After their advancements were rejected, those men went on to stalk and some have even killed the women. This is because they were being tormented by demonic thoughts and were greatly in need of deliverance.

6. Stay where God placed you regardless of how you feel. Think of it this way—you can stay still when your emotions are all over the place or you can move until your emotions settle. If you allow your emotions to control you, you will always be led

outside the will of God by your feelings.

7. Remember that any relationship that is forced is unhealthy and ungodly, but Godly, healthy relationships form when people are on the same paths in Christ and they are of like minds. In other words, if it's God's will for you to have those relationships, they will form in due season.

Lastly, don't allow people to manipulate you into forming soul ties with them. Take your time, pray about everyone who auditions for a role in your life, test the spirit and move in wisdom. You don't owe anyone an apology or an explanation should you choose to not form a relationship with them. Never allow someone to place the weight of their emotional baggage on you. Be kind, be loving, be supportive and be Christ-like. Understand that some people won't give you a choice in the matter. You'll have two options with them: either allow them to form the relationship with you that they want or they'll walk away offended. Let them walk away. Whenever people give you an ultimatum, always choose yourself. After all, people who try to force you to have a relationship with them are often soul-snatchers who see something in you that they want to extract. If you open your heart and your life to them, they will suck you dry before discarding you and then playing the victim. And finally, be bold. I didn't "beat around the bush" with Tom. I didn't feel the need to be super nice and completely disregard the red flags that I saw. That's how people get killed! I tested the spirit, saw that it wasn't of God, and then I proceeded to communicate my boundaries to Tom. He didn't like what I said, nor did he like my boundaries, but I couldn't make that my problem. My job was to simply communicate, solidify and enforce those boundaries, after all, boundary setting is one of the most surefire ways to test a spirit, given the fact that bound people hate boundaries. And again, when you don't dance around with your words, they typically start saying things that do not make sense because they don't know what to do when they are not in control. Take your time and if someone is trying to force you into a relationship (romantic or platonic) or if they are trying to rush into your immediate or intimate circle, shut the door on that person, and if doing so makes you feel bad for that person, try using that empathy on yourself. In other words, stop feeling sorry for people who don't feel sorry for you.

Relational Weights

Every word has weight. Every conversation has weight. Every thought has weight. Every belief has weight. Everything that we say has weight. There are light conversations and there are heavy ones. This is important because not everyone can bear the weight of your words. Some people need light, not so deep conversations, while others need heavy-hitting, in-depth conversations to retain their interests. Think about it like this—if you sit down and attempt to talk with the average three-year old about politics, that child will doze off on you. This is because a conversation about democrats, republicans, liberals, conservatives and the like would be incredibly boring to a toddler. All the same, the conversation would go above the child's understanding and it would be too broad for the child's intellectual capacity. The reason this is important is because we have a tendency to burden people with our words and thoughts. We have a habit of weighing people down with our issues. I can honestly say that I was one of those people who didn't realize just how heavy my words can be. Over time, I had to learn to:

1. Start light. Gauge where a person is before having an extensive conversation with the person.
2. Change the weight of my words if the person shows signs of stress or discomfort. For example, I had to learn to change the topic if the individual puts me on hold, changes the subject, becomes unusually quiet, becomes triggered (angry) or starts showing

excessive pity when I'm speaking on a particular subject. For some people, I had to go deeper and talk about heavier matters; for others, I had to talk about lighter matters.

3. Make a mental notation of any and every conversation I'd had with a person that made the person behave oddly during or after the conversation. In this, I had to ask questions if I didn't know what I'd said to make the person uncomfortable or, in some cases, I'd just mentally revisit the conversation and try to gauge when a shift took place. Sometimes, the issue is a person sees you a certain way. For example, some people may see you as invincible; to them, you may be immortal, and the minute they speak with you, they realize that you're just as human and flawed as they are. From there, they begin to become controlling towards you or avoidant of you. In cases like these, you've given the person something that was either too heavy or too sacred for the individual to hold. In this, I would apologize for having the conversation with the person, and I wouldn't allow the person to drag me back into that topic. I'd keep everything surface-level from that point on.

4. Reevaluate the circle I've placed the person in if the conversation leads to disrespectful behavior, gossip, slander or the like.

5. Pay attention to the weight of words a person gives me. If everything the person is discussing with me is surface-level, I've learned to keep my words light and airy.

It is important to note that you can dig in conversation, and what I mean by this is—you can start off having a surface-level conversation with a person, and then slowly navigate into deeper topics. As humans, we have a tendency to do this with the newbies in our lives. This is because, in the beginning, we are establishing the dominant conversation that we'll be having with these folks, and we are also subconsciously gauging what we can say versus what we can't say to them. After we have built somewhat of a relationship with the people in question, we then tend to have default talk. Default talk is nothing but words and subjects that we tend to default to. For example, Charity's default talk with her friend, Becky, may be Christ-centered. So, when Charity calls Becky, the conversation typically starts off with, "Girl, let me tell you what God did today" or "Pray for me, I've been going through a storm lately." When Becky initiates the conversation, however, her default talk may be about men. She may say, "Girl, you wouldn't believe who called me today!" After this, she'd wait for Charity to give her trademark, "Baby girl, who?!" before finishing her statement. "Morris from Human Resources. He tried to act like he didn't see when I'd clocked in, but five minutes into the conversation, he started talking about what he wants in a wife!" Because their default talk is different, the women may avoid one another's calls from time to time. If Charity doesn't want to hear about men, she'll send Becky to voicemail. If Becky doesn't want to talk about Jesus, she'll return the favor.

Most of us are familiar with 2 Corinthians 6:14 (ESV),

which reads, "Do not be unequally yoked with unbelievers. For what partnership has righteousness with lawlessness? Or what fellowship has light with darkness?" First off, what is a yoke? According to Oxford Languages, a yoke is "a wooden crosspiece that is fastened over the necks of two animals and attached to the plow or cart that they are to pull." Paddling Magazine reported, "An ox can pull its own weight, usually between 1,500 and 3,000 pounds. A well-trained team of two can pull up to 12,000 pounds for short distances, according to Lancaster Farming" (Source: Paddling Magazine/ 8 Things You Didn't Know About Yokes). Most discussions about being unequally yoked involve a donkey and an ox. The donkey is obviously smaller and weaker, plus, donkeys are often regarded as stubborn animals. Therefore, when we discuss the concept of being unequally yoked, we liken the ox to the believer and the donkey to the unbeliever. Let's look at a few facts about each animal.

Donkey	Ox
The average adult donkey weighs between 400 and 500 pounds.	Adult oxen typically weigh between 1,500 to 3,000 pounds.
Can carry up to 125 pounds on its back.	Can carry up to 20% of their body weight (roughly 150–300 pounds).
Can pull up to two times its body weight (roughly 800 to 1,000 pounds).	Can pull up to its body weight when alone (1,500–3,000 pounds), but up to 12,000 pounds when paired

Donkey	Ox
	with another ox.
Were considered unclean animals in the Old Testament, even though they could be redeemed with a lamb.	Were considered clean animals in the Old Testament.
Can travel between 4-5 miles per day (while walking, not galloping, and without a load or burden).	Can travel up to 15 miles per day (without a burden).

Again, when we enter the talk about being unequally yoked, believers are compared with oxen, while unbelievers are compared with donkeys, and oxen are often cast as the victims. This is because:

1. The ox will assume more of the weight (responsibility).
2. Donkeys can be relatively emotional, meaning they are often led by how they feel. So, if a donkey doesn't like you or what you're doing, the donkey will refuse to carry out any task that you give it.
3. Donkeys analyze everything; this is why they are considered stubborn, but oxen don't ask questions. Instead, they simply move forward. In other words, they walk by faith. This can, however, get them in trouble, after all, the Bible compares the lust-filled man with an ox being led to its own slaughter in Proverbs 7:22.
4. The ox can and will go further than the standard

donkey on an average day.

This is to say that when we unequally yoke ourselves with unbelievers, we will:
1. Assume the greater responsibility in that relationship.
2. Have to be the more rational one, in most cases.
3. Carry the burden of walking by faith, while the unbeliever panics and makes a lot of noise.
4. Eventually find ourselves alone, carrying the burden by ourselves.
5. Repeatedly have to reduce the weight of our words and conversations to avoid confusion and conflict.

Howbeit, there is another way that we can look at this dynamic, and this time, the ox or believer isn't the victim. The donkey or unbeliever is. How so?
1. The unbeliever will be expected to carry responsibilities, both natural and spiritual, that he or she is not yet equipped to carry.
2. The unbeliever will have to endure the weight of the believer's crushing words, for example, talks of hell, destruction and generational curses.
3. The believer will exalt his or her feelings above the emotions of the unbeliever, especially in discussions about faith. This further breaks the trust of the unbeliever.
4. The unbeliever lacks the ability to understand spiritual things. This will ultimately cause the unbeliever to be forced to perform despite how he or she feels. This not only causes the unbeliever a great deal of trauma, it can also further repel the

unbeliever from Jesus or can lead the unbeliever into a place of deception. By this, I mean, the unbeliever may learn to perform religious acts for the sake of not embarrassing the believer.

5. The unbeliever will be forced to move at the pace of the believer, even though he or she doesn't understand or agree with the believer's faith. Consequently, the unbeliever will often abandon his or her post out of frustration.

Why did I share that particular perspective? Because it is common for believers to chase people away from Christ and then play the victims whenever their love interests go on the run, choosing their sanity over their relationships. Our job is to reconcile unbelievers to Christ, but when we decide to win them to ourselves first, we create the donkey/ox dynamic. And while the donkey may have cheated, been abusive and behaved like a wild ass, the fact of the matter is that the donkey was, quite frankly, acting like a donkey. Think of it this way—a 38-year old man walks into a grocery store and spots a 15-year old girl who happens to be a runaway. Instead of calling the cops, he strikes up a conversation with her while the two are standing in line. He then proceeds to follow her into the parking lot. Thinking he's being fatherly, the young girl does not question his motives. "Are you lost? Where are you about to go?" the man asks. The young girl looks to the left and then to the right before answering. "No, I'm not lost," she says. "I think I'm going to go home." Knowing that the girl is a runaway, the man asks, "Where's home? Can I give you a ride? Or, if you want, you can come and stay with me." The young girl jumps on the opportunity because for the last few days, she'd been sleeping under a bridge. She thinks to herself, "This guy can make my life much better! He has a house, a car and some money to spare." She turns and looks at the guy and says, "Sure, let's go to your house. I don't want to go home. How long can I stay with you?" Excited, the man proclaims, "As long as you want ... daughter!" The two then get into his pickup truck. Let's stop there and consider these facts:

1. If he raises her as his own daughter, he's wrong because she has a family out there that he's keeping her from and helping her to rebel against. The fact is—she's not his daughter, and by hosting her in his home, he may be contributing to the delinquency of a minor which, of course, is a crime within itself.

2. If he decides to carry on an inappropriate relationship with her, he's an evil, twisted and perverted man; I'm sure we can all agree on this.

3. If he allows her to live with him and determine the nature of their relationship, he is a sick and evil man, after all, she's not old enough to make that kind of a decision.

Let's consider another alternative ending. What if the man in question was attracted to the teenager, but because he feared going to jail, plus as a father to a teenager, he'd reasoned within himself that he wouldn't want a 38-year old man robbing his daughter of her innocence, he'd decided to wait until she was 18-years old before attempting to carry on a sexual relationship with the girl?

Sure, conversations like these are not easy to have, but what if the guy groomed her to be his wife by providing a house for her to stay in, food for her to eat and pretty much any and everything she asked for? We'd still consider him a monster, right?! This is because he robbed her of her sobriety; he "captured" her when she was young, rebellious, ignorant and lost, and he exploited the young lady for his own benefit. This would make him a sexual predator, a menace to society and every negative term we could conjure up. Isn't this what we're doing when we romantically soul-tie ourselves to babes in Christ? Isn't this spiritual pedophilia? We have to stop "capturing" babes in Christ, having inappropriate relationships with them, and then playing the victim when they act their ages or stages. Think of it this way—the man in question waits until the young girl turns 18 before marrying her, and it is only then that he touches her for the first time. Three months later, she leaves his house, files for divorce and starts dating a 19-year old former classmate of hers, and when asked about her decision to divorce her now 41-year old husband, she replies, "Cause, he's old and boring" before blowing a huge bubble with her gum and rolling her eyes. Who would be the villain in this story? Some people would argue that they are both wrong, but the truth is, the young lady would simply be acting her age. Her estranged husband would be the villain in this story, no matter how we tried to decorate his behavior. Again, this is what it looks like when we go after men and women who, biblically speaking, are babes in Christ. A lot of unbelievers are chased away from the faith, not just by big-hat wearing rejects sitting on the front rows of their local assemblies;

they are chased away from the church by seasoned believers who saw their potential and tried to get them off the market before they matured. Let's face it. This is the same behavior that we see some young ladies exhibiting when they are in high school or college, and one of the young boys on the basketball or football team starts showing NFL or NBA potential. They throw themselves at these young men, hoping to have babies with these guys. This behavior is so common that it is often depicted in films. Christian men and women do this! They see a babe in Christ's potential, and from there, they try to soul-tie themselves to these new believers while they are still impressionable and immature. They get married, have children, and four years later, you'll find them live on YouTube referring to their estranged partners as "narcissists" when, in truth, some of these folks were simply acting their ages, spiritually speaking. I'm saying this so that we can stop playing the victims in stories where we were the villains. "If anyone causes one of these little ones—those who believe in me—to stumble, it would be better for them to have a large millstone hung around their neck and to be drowned in the depths of the sea" (Matthew 18:6). Imagine it this way. Phyllis dates and marries a man that she'd met at her local bar. Phyllis is Christian; she is also a minister at her church and a self-proclaimed evangelist.

One day, Phyllis goes into a bar to minister to some of the people in the place, but things didn't go exactly as planned. "What can I get you to drink?" the bartender asks. He happens to be the epitome of tall, dark and handsome.

Phyllis is taken aback. She's never seen a more handsome man in her life. It takes Phyllis a few seconds before she's gathered herself enough to answer the beautiful stranger's question. "I'll have a virgin margarita," she says. The bartender looks at the petite brunet in disappointment. "What, no alcohol?" he asks. Phyllis admires his pearly white teeth all the more. "I wonder if he's wearing dentures," she thinks to herself. "After all, there's no way his teeth are that perfect. Heck, his whole face is perfect!" Realizing that he's being admired, the bartender smiles all the more, revealing his two incredibly deep dimples and a set of perfectly chiseled smile lines. "I don't drink alcohol," Phyllis replies, smiling sheepishly at the bartender. Before the night ends, Phyllis exchanges numbers with Brice, the bartender, and the two begin building a friendship. Phyllis can clearly see Brice's potential. The son and grandson of pastors, Brice's future looks heavenly. "Maybe I'm the one God sent to win his soul back to Christ," Phyllis reasons with herself. Brice's mother agrees wholeheartedly. She's been praying for her son to return to Christ for more than a decade, so Phyllis' emergence in his life, to his mother, seems to be orchestrated by Heaven. Howbeit, Brice has absolutely no desire to return to Christ. Not wanting to follow in his father's footsteps, Brice has done everything to disqualify himself from the ministry, including publicly attacking his estranged father on social media. The problem is, even though Brice was raised in the church, he was not raised in Christ. You see, neither his father or grandfather truly knew God; they knew religion, and because they didn't have an intimate relationship with God, they'd done every wild thing they once preached against while serving in ministry. So, anytime Phyllis talks about church and Christ, Brice attempts to end the conversation by changing the subject, getting off the phone or becoming argumentative. Not willing to back down or give up, Phyllis continues to pursue the brown-eyed bartender. Why? Because she can see his potential! If Brice gave his life to Christ, he'd not only be a handsome man of God that all of the women at the church would wish upon a star for, he'd also be a powerful man of God, given his testimony. Phyllis regularly imagines Brice standing on a pulpit, casting out devils and sharing his testimony with an awestruck crowd. In her fantasies, he'd invite her onto the stage to tell the world how she had been the only woman, outside of his mother, who believed in him enough to fight for his soul. He'd propose to her in front of a crowd of thousands and the two of them would go on to have the wedding of the century. This wedding would be followed by a few dimple-faced kids and a life of luxury. A year later, the two marry in a small church ceremony, and even though Phyllis hadn't gotten the proposal she wanted, she is convinced that her new husband will be a star someday, and he'd radiate the love of God upon her in front of a large crowd. This never happens. What does happen, however, is Phyllis repeatedly crushes her husband with her words. In turn, he crushes her expectations of him, plus he's a promiscuous man who uses his bar-tending job as an excuse to stay out late and entertain other women. Three years and two kids later, Brice has had enough. "You keep saying that I'm going to hell if I don't change my life, but dear Phyllis, I went to hell when I married you," he rants. After their divorce is final,

Phyllis goes online to share her testimony. She concludes her podcast with these words, "That's my story, guys! That's what it's like to be married to a narcissist. God delivered me from that clown, and even though he's a decent father, that man tried to destroy me!" The light dims in the studio as Phyllis opens the line for questions. What did you witness in this fiasco? You literally witnessed an event that is commonplace today. Phyllis went after a babe in Christ who may have very well been her assignment, just not her husband. Then again, maybe Brice wasn't her assignment; he was her test or, better yet, her temptation. He was the proverbial Ishmael who'd surfaced before Isaac, but Phyllis had been so distracted by his good looks that she'd failed to examine his character. After this, she unwittingly allowed Satan to use her to drive her husband further and further away from Christ. Now, every encounter Brice has had with someone claiming to be a Christian has been not only negative, but it was traumatizing. Some people would argue—wait, he's the cheater?! How is he traumatized when he's the villain?! Please understand that it is possible (and common) for people to find themselves in a villain on villain relationship! It is possible for Jezebel to marry Jezebel, just like it's possible for Ahab to marry Ahab. These homo-spiritual relationships are often misdiagnosed because we've been tamed and trained to believe that anytime you find a villain in a relational dynamic, the other person involved absolutely has to be the victim. So, when we see a covert narcissist married to an overt narcissist, we have a tendency to side with the covert, not realizing that playing the hero in a villain on villain relationship is the quickest way to become a victim, after all, every villain needs a victim and every victim is developed by a villain. Therefore, whenever you come across a homo-spiritual relationship, please understand that you are volunteering to be the seed-bearer in that relationship. What this means is— Jezebel needs an Ahab to carry out her sinister plans, and if you come upon a Jezebel-on-Jezebel relationship, your interference in that relationship could easily render you as Jezebel's newest Ahab. You may find yourself ministering to the covert narcissist because that individual is soft-spoken and relatively shy, unlike his loud, overbearing and vengeful wife. Howbeit, neither of the two is a victim; they are both diabolical, manipulative and controlling.

A lot of believers today prefer to believe that Phyllis will go to Heaven, and the pearly gates will open for her, while Brice falls so hard into the pits of hell that he breaks the sound barrier there. What may end up happening, however, is that Brice eventually has an encounter with Christ, but Phyllis descends into bitterness until she eventually lifts up her eyes in hell. This is to say that we should never underestimate the weight and the power of our words and choices, especially when we come in contact with wild asses (unbelievers).

I was talking over the phone with a relative of mine one day. This particular relative is not saved (we'll call him Ron). Ron talks about God, but most of what he says comes from a hurt place. All the same, Ron and I don't talk often. We typically speak maybe once or twice a year. We started talking about spiritual things, and I heard the Lord tell me not to tell Ron what demon he had in him. Ron has a bad habit of cutting me off any time I'm talking, and he always says, "I don't mean to cut you off, but ..." From there, he'll start challenging what I'm saying or changing the topic. I spoke for a minute or so before Ron cut me off. "I don't mean to cut you off, but what demon do you think I have in me?" I paused. I could hear God's voice again. "Don't say that." Did I listen to the Lord? No, I didn't. I listed what I believed Ron needed to be delivered from, and oh my! I didn't anticipate what would happen next. Ron's voice got loud; his anger rose to the top and he started twisting my words. I could barely keep up with what he was saying. I sat there, nodded my head and allowed him to go off, while I beat myself up for not obeying God. I tried to interrupt and explain what I meant, but Ron wasn't having it. He kept yelling and saying the most confusing things. That's it. I had no choice but to say yet another benediction to Ron, knowing full-well that it would probably be another year before I spoke with him again. "I'm sorry," I said, hoping that my apology would make things right between Ron and I, but it didn't. The issue is—what I'd told Ron was too heavy for him. I was, without question, in error, not just because God told me not to say what I said, but because Ron isn't saved. He doesn't understand spiritual things, but my desire to save him had gotten the best of me. Obviously, for a moment, I thought I knew better than God. I didn't. I chased Ron further into the pain that he'd come to associate with Christians and Christianity. Have I repented? Yes, of course, but I can't undo the damage that has been done. All I can do is pray for Ron and hope that he'll someday be reconciled with Christ in this lifetime. What I'm saying is—

what I shared with Ron was way too heavy for him. To him, I was judging him. To him, I didn't like or care about him, but in truth, I was hoping that Ron would hear what I said and desire deliverance. I learned a lot in that moment, but one of the most important lessons, outside of the fact that I need to obey God in all things, was—people often ask for information that is too weighty for them, but we, as believers, shouldn't give it to them just because they ask for it. After all, we ask God for a lot, but He doesn't release those things to us until we have enough faith to bear what we're asking for. Even a blessing can crush you if you're not anchored in the Word of God.

Every personality has weight. Some people's personalities are too strong for others, while some people's personalities are too forceful for others. They are not one and the same. If a person's personality is too strong for you, the individual may not have much give, meaning the individual states what he or she believes and isn't willing to consider any alternatives. A person with a forceful personality, on the other hand, wrestles with the spirit of control, and that individual will try to force his or her beliefs on you. The individual in question will even try to force you to do what he or she wants you to do. How is a strong personality different from a forceful one? A strong personality is backed by knowledge and some degree of understanding about a specific topic. Simply put, the individual is convinced that what he or she is telling you is right. Now, it doesn't mean that the individual is right; it simply means that the individual believes that what he or she is sharing with you is correct information. A forceful personality is backed by pride and some degree of knowledge. Simply put, the individual has heard or learned a tidbit of information, drafted a conclusion using that information, and now the individual is trying to force that information on you. Forceful personalities and strong personalities sound the same in a general conversation or a heated debate, but when presented with facts or information that challenges their views, they respond differently. Someone who has a strong personality will consider the information if it is accredited or credible; someone who is prideful will not consider the information, but will instead become offended and attempt to end the conversation or the individual may resort to name-calling or violence.

Of course, there are people who are meek, meaning their temperaments are not that strong. Meek-mannered people tend to avoid forceful personalities because people who are forceful often eclipse their personalities with their own, thus causing the meek to feel muzzled and controlled. Some meek-mannered people will also avoid people with strong personalities because meek-mannered people have too much give, meaning they'll constantly compromise and give people what they want, thus repeatedly robbing themselves of their own voices and desires. All the same, this could easily become the culture in a relationship and set the stage for the Jezebel/Ahab dynamic if the souls involved are not healthy. However, you will notice healthy relationships that involve meek people and strong-willed people. The two will typically balance one another out or, if they are not healthy, cancel one another out. I tend to be a mixture of both; I am strong-willed in the areas that I'm confident, but I can be mild or meek-mannered in other areas. This is why I understand Apostle Paul's message when he said in Philippians 4:12, "I know both how to be abased, and I know how to abound: every where and in all things I am instructed both to be full and to be hungry, both to abound and to suffer need." That's how relational intelligence works. It's knowing when to speak up versus when to be silent; it's knowing when you're the teacher versus when you're the student. It's also knowing and appreciating the fact that a student can teach the teacher a lesson. Another way to say this is—God often hides revelation in low places. He hides wisdom in places where we wouldn't think to look; this way, we have to humble ourselves to get that information. He'll hide wisdom in a child, a homeless man or a drug-addicted woman. He'll hide revelation in a pagan woman, a mentally ill man or a serial killer. Don't get me wrong; these people may not be continuous streams of revelation and good information, but in any given moment, they may look at you and say something that could potentially save your life, and if you're too prideful to hear them, you could pay dearly for your stubbornness. For example, a homeless man could see you walking with a group of people and say, "They're not your friends, ma'am." A woman may see you in the club and say, "You don't belong here."

There are two things you can do to increase your relational acumen, and they are:
1. Listen more than you speak.
2. Pay attention more than you require attention.

Learn the texture of your personality in every area of your life, and pay attention to how everyone responds to you in those areas. For example, how strong are you when you enter a discussion about finances? Are you silent, uninformed or passive, or do you lead those conversations? What about family matters? How strong are you in this particular area of your life? What about romance? Are you versed in Godly romance or worldly romance, and are you a novice, advanced beginner or an expert? The old folks used to say, "An empty wagon makes a lot of noise." This expression means that a person who knows very little typically has a lot to say. In conclusion, it is important that you:

1. Not put more on an individual than he or she can bear; this includes expectations and demands.
2. Be relationally flexible. Know the weight of your words and the capacity of the people in your life; this way, you'll know how to have healthy, flourishing and Godly relationships with those people.
3. Take accountability for your role in your own pain, especially if that pain came as the result of you placing a huge expectation on an unbeliever or an immature believer. Also, repent for spiritual pedophilia if you've involved yourself in it.
4. Know the weight or strength of your personality; this way, you won't repeatedly overburden people with your presence.
5. Learn how to be soft and when to be hard. In other words, learn how to read a room.
6. Know the weight of your pain, understanding that

not everyone can bear what you've been trusted to carry. This is why wise counsel is important. Having wise counselors gives you an outlet for your pain with men and women who know what to do with that pain, versus you burdening your mother, your best friend or your spouse with pain that they are not equipped to carry.

7. Know the weight of your presence. Some people don't necessarily dislike you; you may have a commanding presence that makes them feel small and intimidated. You can't do anything about the weight of your presence, but having relational acumen will help you to identify people who may feel overwhelmed when you're around; this way, you will know how to approach and address them.

8. Know the weight of your love. Believe it or not, there are some people who have yet to receive the love of God, and they haven't received a healthy measure of love from people. Consequently, the more love you give them, the more they'll sabotage their relationships with you. This is because your love may be too much for them; they don't understand it, nor do they trust it. They need God's love, and with His love comes joy. The joy of the Lord is our strength. Once they have allowed God to arrest them with His love, they will be strong and wise enough to bear the love of others.

9. Know the weight of your testimonies. I soon learned that not everyone could bear the weight of my testimonies. This is why the word "triggered" seems to be trending today. You'll notice that some people

will post a video sharing their stories, but before they start sharing their testimonies, they'll say, "Trigger warning." This is because a lot of people are still in pain as a result of something they themselves have undergone or some people are too sensitive to hear about what another person has gone through. I had to learn to share a light testimony before sharing a heavier one. This is my way of gauging the capacity and strength of the listener.

10. Know the weight of God's Word. Never place your opinion, your degree, your education, what you've heard or what you've come to believe over God's Word. People who make this mistake often become enemies of the faith, exalting man's knowledge over God's Word. Their stories all end the same. If they don't repent, they spend the rest of their lives wrestling with bitterness.

COGNITIVE INTELLIGENCE VS. SPIRITUAL INTELLIGENCE

First, let's talk about cognitive intelligence. According to the American Psychological Association's Dictionary of Psychology, cognitive intelligence is "one's ability to learn, remember, reason, solve problems, and make sound judgments, particularly as contrasted with emotional intelligence." Have you ever heard the saying, "Common sense isn't common?" In truth, I thought I'd personally coined that adage back around 2005 or 2006 when I'd posted it to a Black Voices message board, but as the years passed, I've heard it spoken by people all over the world. I remember seeing other people post that phrase, and in one or two instances, I sprung forward to claim the statement. Nevertheless, after hearing the statement time and time again, I had to utilize one of the lowest forms of cognitive intelligence, and that is what we call "common sense." What did common sense tell me? Great minds truly do think alike! What I mean by this is—a good idea or thought isn't necessarily an original one. Another definition of cognitive intelligence comes from Mercer:

> "Cognitive intelligence is referred to as human mental ability and understanding developed through thinking, experiences and senses. It is the ability to generate knowledge by using existing information. It also includes other intellectual functions such as attention, learning, memory, judgment and reasoning.

Cognitive intelligence is the ability of the human brain to digest information and form intelligence and meaning. Hence, measuring cognitive intelligence is crucial for organizations undertaking recruitment, as it determines whether an applicant has the aptitude to perform well at work that requires significant cognitive ability. It is said that cognitive intelligence uses existing knowledge that grows with practice and different experiences" (Source: Mercer/ www.mettl.com/ Glossary/ Cognitive Intelligence).

I'd been running Anointed Fire Magazine for a few months when this incident took place. The incident itself was not grand or major; in truth, it was anticlimactic, at best, but it has ministered to me over the years. We were one to two days away from launching our next edition, and I was frustrated because some of the writers had not yet sent in their articles. I was mainly frustrated with the major writers; these were the people who had featured spots in the magazine. I reached out to one of the women to inquire about her article. I'll never forget her response. She said, "I haven't written anything because God hasn't given me anything." I let out a loud sigh before responding. I told her something to the effect of, "I understand, but you should have revelation stored in your belly from your experiences and your encounters with God. Every article doesn't have to be prophetic in nature. Draw from what you already have." In other words, when God is silent, it's because He's given us enough wisdom and revelation through His Word and through our experiences that we can draw from. So, if I challenged you to write a book about anxiety, you should be able to start and finish that book if you've had a mild to extensive history with anxiety. You wouldn't have to wait for God to tell you what to say. Thankfully, those words encouraged the writer, and a few hours later, she sent in a really good article. What I'm saying is—your cognitive intelligence grows as you continue to experience life, but your spiritual intelligence grows as you continue to experience God. I grew to realize that a large portion of my faith comes from my history with God.

Spiritual intelligence is comprised of:
1. Your knowledge of God's Word.
2. Your understanding of God's Word.
3. Your revelation of God's Word.
4. Your history with God's enemy (warfare chronicles).
5. Your history with God.

Understand that everything that materializes in our lives is a reflection of what's going on in the realm of the spirit. The spirit realm is very active, even when we're passive and inactive. This is why the Bible tells us to pray without ceasing. Consider the plight of Daniel. Daniel 10:1–14 reads, "In the third year of Cyrus king of Persia a word was revealed to Daniel, who was named Belteshazzar. And the word was true, and it was a great conflict. And he understood the word and had understanding of the vision. In those days I, Daniel, was mourning for three weeks. I ate no delicacies, no meat or wine entered my mouth, nor did I anoint myself at all, for the full three weeks. On the twenty-fourth day of the first month, as I was standing on the bank of the great river (that is, the Tigris) I lifted up my eyes and looked, and behold, a man clothed in linen, with a belt of fine gold from Uphaz around his waist. His body was like beryl, his face like the appearance of lightning, his eyes like flaming torches, his arms and legs like the gleam of burnished bronze, and the sound of his words like the sound of a multitude. And I, Daniel, alone saw the vision, for the men who were with me did not see the vision, but a great trembling fell upon them, and they fled to hide themselves. So I was left alone and saw this great vision, and no strength was left in me. My radiant appearance was fearfully changed, and I retained no strength. Then I heard the sound of his words, and as I heard the sound of his words, I fell on my face in deep sleep with my face to the ground. And behold, a hand touched me and set me trembling on my hands and knees. And he said to me, 'O Daniel, man greatly loved, understand the words that I speak to you, and stand upright, for now I have been sent to you.' And when he had spoken this word to me, I stood up trembling. Then he said to me, 'Fear not, Daniel, for from the first day that you set your heart to understand and humbled yourself before your God, your words have been heard, and I have come because of your words. The prince of the kingdom of Persia withstood me twenty-one days, but Michael, one of the chief princes, came to help me, for I was left there with the kings of Persia, and came to make you understand what is to happen to your people in the latter days. For the vision is for days yet to come.'" You see, what Daniel was experiencing in the natural was a reflection of what had been taking place in the realm of the spirit. This is why spiritual intelligence is important.

Another example of spiritual intelligence is something I experienced with God. I used to pray, whine and complain to Him about the man I was married to, and most of those "cry sessions" would end with Him saying, "I know how you feel." I would immediately feel convicted (not condemned) because I realized what God was saying to me. He was letting me know that the very things I'd complained to Him about regarding my significant other were the very things I'd been taking God through. My most memorable "cry session" took place in front of my kitchen sink in the middle of the night. A lot of my time with God took place in that spot. I cried as I washed the dishes, feeling completely sorry for myself. "God, that man doesn't love me. He only wants what he can get out of me. He gives all of his attention to everyone except me." My cry was heartfelt; my heart was hurting, and more than anything, I wanted God's sympathy. Well, He wasn't about to pity me because He saw that moment as an opportunity to teach me so that I could continue to grow in my relationship with Him. "I know how you feel," He said. Like a hurricane, His words, albeit few, spiraled through my victimhood, completely shattering every defense and excuse I had. Suddenly, I found myself naked before Him, with the cloak of victimhood nowhere to be seen. I wasn't the victim. I was reaping what I'd continually been sowing, and I didn't like my harvest. In short, I didn't understand how the spirit realm worked so I was like that naive kid that tried to tickle a cactus, only to discover the meaning behind the old adage, "The same thing that makes you laugh will also make you cry." The more I came to understand spiritual principles, the more intentional I became. I remember waking up and acknowledging that I was reaping the seeds I'd sown, and I said to myself, "I don't want to reap this mess anymore!" From there, I started intentionally sowing good seeds, and I avoided sowing bad ones as well. This means that I had entered a new season; I was no longer high off the lies that the enemy told me. I was sober enough to recognize that I wasn't a victim. I was a harvester who had a history of sowing bad seeds, thinking that they would someday produce blessings because I'd sowed those seeds with good intentions. How deceived I was!

You are multidimensional; we've already established this. Every side of you has a heart (mind) and every mind has a capacity. Of course, you have a single heart in your body, but when we start dealing with the makeup of your soul (mind, will and emotions), we are dealing with a multiplex. Your soul looks like a building with many rooms. Some rooms are filled with the revelation of God, therefore, God reigns over those areas of your soul, while other rooms are dark. Again, a dark room or a dark space in the soul is called a void. The amount of light (revelation) you have in each room determines the amount of access you have to those rooms. For example, if your father was absent or neglectful, in your parental state, you will have wrestled with a void. If you had a father-figure, you would have a measure of light in that room. If you allow YAHWEH to enter that space, He will fill that room. This is why David said in Psalm 27:10, "When my father and my mother forsake me, then the Lord will take me up." Each room has a capacity, but you can't utilize the fullness of that room if it isn't fully illuminated. This means that there are blessings in every room. All the same, the room is the container of your potent al, and your potential consists of all of the gifts and information that God has hidden in each room. Howbeit, you have to seek God (first) if you want to illuminate or tap into your potential.

Again, each room has a heart; the heart of a room is the throne of that room. It is the core belief of that particular neighborhood of thinking; it is the principle that sets the stage for other principles (beliefs). If God is on the throne, the heart is healthy. If the room is dark and void of God, that area of your soul will be unhealthy, and in many cases, demonized. Don't get me wrong; it's not only the lack of information that attracts demonic spirits. What allows them in is when you come into agreement with them, allowing something evil and sinister to move into that room and sit on the throne. This is because there's little to no light there, meaning there's little to no truth in that space. You can also sit on the throne in any given room; this is what we call selfishness, self-worship or self-idolatry. Another word for this is carnality. For example, there are a lot of believers and unbelievers who worship worldly information. Many of them are what we call brainiacs. They learn as much as they can because they like being right, not righteous. Anytime we place ourselves on the throne in any given room and we feed that room a lot of worldly information, a mild or dim light will begin to emit. This is because some information, while not spiritual in nature, is good information. For example, knowledge of how the body functions is good information if what you're taking in is factual. All good information or good things come from God, and they must move through people to get to you and I. Howbeit, the light won't be enough for you to see your way around that space. It'll be enough to keep you from falling. By falling, I mean that some of the info can keep you from making a lot of poor choices. This is why you won't find a lot of gynecologists who engage in promiscuity, and you won't find a lot of lawyers readily breaking the law.

Whatever you place on any given throne has an appetite. If you place God on the throne, you will hunger all the more for His Word, and you will be filled. You will find yourself in bookstores looking for more Christian books, just as you will find yourself online watching Christian videos, reading Christian articles and learning all you can about Christ. If a demonic spirit is on the throne in any given room, that spirit will have an appetite. For example, if the spirit of rejection is on the throne, you will find yourself strongly desiring the attention, acceptance and love of others. This will undoubtedly cause you to run past love's speed limit, thus causing you to attract narcissists and broken people, all the while repelling Godly people. This sets the stage for you to experience more rejection, thus increasing the size of the void and allowing the spirit of rejection to grow until it consumes you. If you place yourself on the throne, you will become more and more self-centered, religious and intolerable. You may even become incredibly ambitious. The way Satan steals this throne from you is by offering you an opportunity (job, relationship, platform). He allows you to sample whatever it is that you want, thus helping you to develop an appetite for that thing. This is the same method or wile that drug dealers use to get people hooked on their drugs. They will give out free samples until their victims are addicted to whatever it is that they're offering, and that's when they'll start charging them to access those drugs. Satan employs the same tactic; he'll send, for example, a love interest into your life, and in the beginning of your relationship with that person, you'll notice that the individual is giving you his or her undivided attention, but the moment you get hooked (soul-tied), a shift will take place. The individual that you've soul-tied yourself to will request and require that you abdicate the throne so that they can sit on it. This request sounds like, "You're selfish" or "All you do is think about yourself!" And get this, the individual is not lying, but spiritually speaking, the spirit in that individual wants that seat. As a matter of fact, it's demanding that seat. This makes me think of one of my mother's ex-boyfriends. We'll call him Angus. I didn't like Angus at all. No one in my family liked Angus. He was a five-time divorcee who'd managed to convince somebody to ordain him as a pastor. No worries. Angus didn't pastor any churches; he simply went to the prisons and served as a pastor there. Angus was not living for the Lord at all. He'd told my mom that he could not sleep with her on Saturday nights because he had to preach on Sundays. He was only abstinent one day out of the week. Additionally, Angus had anger issues. It was reported that he'd abused all of his wives. We tried to warn my mother, but she wouldn't hear of it. "He's not bad!" she'd say in her meek voice. But, Angus was a bad man and we often wondered how long it would be before my mother sobered up to see what everyone else could clearly see. Of course, my mother started idolizing her relationship with Angus, but she hadn't fully gotten into the space where she'd idolized Angus. Yes, people can idolize a relationship without idolizing the person they are in a relationship with in the same way that some women (and men) idolize weddings but want nothing to do with the responsibilities of being married.

One day, my mother jump-started the vehicle that would ultimately drive Angus out of her life. She started looking for her first home. She had been renting all of her life, and now, she was ready to buy a house. Angus was living with (and brandishing his teeth at) his mother. I know this because my Mom told me that Angus did not have a good relationship with his mother. He hadn't moved in with us because we were all living with my aunt. This particular aunt was on her death bed, and my Mom moved in with her to take care of her. So, she allowed Angus to visit her there, but she wouldn't let him move in. However, the moment she got into the market for a house, Angus insisted on tagging along so that he could give his input, after all, in his mind, the house would be his as well. And no, he wasn't contributing a single dime towards the house. My Mom finally found a house that she wanted to buy, and when she was about to start the paperwork for that house, Angus insisted that she put his name on the house as well. Understand this—every deity requires offerings, and not just spiritual ones, they require natural ones as well. My mother made me proud when she refused to put his name on her house. Angus insisted, but my mother stood her ground. Feeling the impact of his narcissistic injury, Angus broke up with my mother. She was heartbroken, but she didn't compromise her position in an attempt to win him back. My mother would go on to get into another relationship with another broken man, and she let him move into her new home with her. This guy would live with her for eight years, bumming off her and being completely disrespectful towards her. I remember this guy (we'll call him Clancy) saying to me, "I don't know where your sister is going to go when your mother dies because she can't live here!" He would say the same about my brother, and he'd said this to a few of the people in my family. Howbeit, I'd convinced them to not say a word because it was clear to me that Clancy thought that living with my mother would somehow override the written will she had in place, and I didn't want him to know the truth. If he had known the truth, I was afraid that he'd use his relationship and proximity to my mother to get her to change her will or, at minimum, he'd marry her. Don't mistake what I'm saying; my Mom didn't have a lot to leave behind. The house she was buying was not in good condition. Nevertheless, Clancy wasn't going to sex his way into becoming a homeowner. My mother ended her relationship with Clancy about nine years before she passed away, so his not-so-ingenious plans to become a homeowner/squatter were foiled. The point I'm making here is this—when you are on the throne of any given room, Satan will send people to take that throne from you so that he can sit on it.

Again, whatever you place on any given throne has an

appetite; this appetite is what we call your capacity. You can have God on a throne, but not have that great of an appetite in that room simply because you're still young in the faith in that area, meaning you're still a babe in Christ. Babes don't hunger for revelation; they hunger for what they'd been fed in Egypt (sin). Because of this, babes tend to fill themselves with false information (lies) and the doctrines of devils. This is why there are so many Christians engaging in New Age practices. If you keep feeding yourself ungodly information, you will essentially evict God from the throne, thus opening yourself to unclean spirits. My objective here is to show you why you are attracted to the information that you tend to fill yourself with. All the same, the info you attract will attract people to you as it establishes principles, and principles are the ties responsible for linking souls together.

Your experience in the natural should never be used to discredit the spirit realm. Cognitive intelligence is great, but it does not and can never replace or outrank spiritual intelligence. This is why it is sad to see Christians get degrees and then think they're smart enough to challenge the Bible, all the while still referring to themselves as Christians. I can honestly say that I've noticed a pattern with a lot of believers who've followed this dark path, and that pattern is—they slowly descend into double-mindedness; that is until they reach the point of no return. By this, I mean that they renounce Christ and use their history with the church to challenge the Bible. God gives them space to repent, but they refuse to do so.

Consequently, they are suddenly tossed into the ring with Jezebel (the narcissist). Revelation 2:20-22 reads, "Notwithstanding I have a few things against thee, because thou sufferest that woman Jezebel, which calleth herself a prophetess, to teach and to seduce my servants to commit fornication, and to eat things sacrificed unto idols. And I gave her space to repent of her fornication; and she repented not. Behold, I will cast her into a bed, and them that commit adultery with her into great tribulation, except they repent of their deeds." Note, this has everything to do with ambition. You see, some people don't want God; instead, they want what He has to offer, but God requires us to be processed before we can get our hands on some of the things we desire. This is so that those things don't become idols. When ambitious Christians go out into the world, Satan offers them all of what they've prayed for or some of what they've prayed for in exchange for their testimonies against God's bride (the church). Realizing that the world is at their fingerprints, many of them believed that they no longer needed God, thus proving that their pursuit of Him had been centered around selfish gain. They shake hands with the devil the moment they come against God's people, thus initiating their descent into madness. This downward spiral usually looks like them challenging the church, getting a little attention, finding themselves in demonic relationships (oftentimes with Jezebel) and losing everything that they once cherished, including the respect of the people who once praised them. The more they lose, the angrier with God they become; this causes them to challenge Him more, thus setting the stage for an even greater plummet into nothingness, followed by more demonic encounters. They get angrier, thus growing more and more evil and setting the stage for more devils to enter their souls. This declination looks like them falling into the bottomless pit while they are still yet alive. Before long, you'll find them claiming to be or supporting witches, warlocks, sorcerers and satanists. This spiritual vortex drags them further and further into the darkness until they become yet another forgotten memory on Earth. I've seen prophets and prophetic people plunge into this sinkhole, oftentimes because they want what the world has to offer and they want little to nothing to do with their assignments; that is unless their assignments place them in spotlights. Consider what happened with Jonah.

- **Jonah 1:1-3:** Now the word of the LORD came unto Jonah the son of Amittai, saying, Arise, go to Nineveh, that great city, and cry against it; for their wickedness is come up before me. But Jonah rose up to flee unto Tarshish from the presence of the LORD, and went down to Joppa; and he found a ship going to Tarshish: so he paid the fare thereof, and went down into it, to go with them unto Tarshish from the presence of the LORD.

Jonah attempted to run from the call on his life. Unlike many prophets, he had not only been called, but he'd been chosen to carry out an assignment. Jonah didn't want the backlash that came with being a prophet, so he attempted to run from the Most High God. How did this end?

- **Jonah 1:4-17:** But the LORD sent out a great wind into the sea, and there was a mighty tempest in the sea, so that the ship was like to be broken. Then the mariners were afraid, and cried every man unto his god, and cast forth the wares that were in the ship into the sea, to lighten it of them. But Jonah was gone down into the sides of the ship; and he lay, and was fast asleep. So the shipmaster came to him, and said unto him, What meanest thou, O sleeper? Arise, call upon thy God, if so be that God will think upon us, that we perish not. And they said every one to his fellow, Come, and let us cast lots, that we may know for whose cause this evil is upon us. So they cast lots, and the lot fell upon Jonah. Then said they unto him, Tell us, we pray thee, for whose cause this evil is upon us; What is thine occupation? and whence comest thou? What is thy country? And of what people art thou? And he said unto them, I am an Hebrew; and I fear the LORD, the God of heaven, which hath made the sea and the dry land. Then were the men exceedingly afraid, and said unto him, Why hast thou done this? For the men knew that he fled from the presence of the LORD, because he had told them. Then said they unto him, What shall we do unto thee, that the sea may be calm unto us? For the sea wrought, and was tempestuous. And he said unto them, Take me up, and cast me forth into the sea; so shall the sea be calm unto you: for I know that for my sake this great tempest is upon you. Nevertheless the men rowed hard to bring it to the land; but they could not: for the sea wrought, and was tempestuous against them. Wherefore they cried unto the LORD, and said, We beseech thee, O LORD, we beseech thee, let us not perish for this man's life, and lay not upon us innocent blood: for thou, O LORD, hast done as it pleased thee. So they took up Jonah, and cast him forth into the sea: and the sea ceased from her raging. Then the men feared the LORD exceedingly, and offered a sacrifice unto the LORD, and made vows. Now the LORD had prepared a great fish to swallow up Jonah. And Jonah was in the belly of the fish three days and three nights.

Here, we see that Jonah's decision to run from God provoked God to stir up the sea. The men were about to lose their lives simply because they shared the same space as Jonah. And notice that Jonah didn't consider repenting at that time. Instead, he asked the men to toss him into the sea, meaning he would rather be dead than to be a prophet. Howbeit, after spending three days in the great fish's belly, Jonah had a change of heart. Jonah 2 details Jonah's prayer, and it ends with the great fish vomiting Jonah out on dry land. The great fish in this story, believe it or not, was Leviathan, a great serpent and fish that lived in the ocean. Today, Leviathan is also regarded as an unclean spirit. Check out the following article about Leviathan:

> "The Leviathan is a Biblical sea monster, a mythical creature referred to in sections of the Old Testament, and while a popular metaphor in both Judaism and Christianity, the creature nonetheless is viewed differently in each religion. The creature can either be seen as a metaphor for

the sheer size and power of God's creative abilities, or a demonic beast. In this context, the Leviathan is regarded as the monster of the waters, while the Behemoth and the Ziz are regarded as monsters of the earth and the air, respectively. Outside of religion, leviathan has become synonymous with any large sea creature, particularly whales" (Source: New World Encyclopedia/Leviathan).

Jonah didn't understand that being chosen by God wasn't the same as being called by Him. All prophets are called by God, but few are chosen by Him. Understand that you can be called and still carry out your assignment in the Earth, but when God has something significant that He wants to be done, He will often choose a prophet to carry out the assignment. Today, there are many prophets in mental hospitals, marriages with Jezebel or in the pits of sin because they chose normality over their assignments, not realizing that resisting God places them outside of His will. God is Light; the Bible tells us this. This means that in order for us to hide from Him, we would have to go outside His will, and ever then, He knows where we are, after all He is omnipresent (in all places at once), omniscient (all-knowing) and omnipotent (all powerful). Outside of God's will is darkness since He is Light, and the prince of darkness (Satan) is the ruler of the dark world. So, going outside of God's will places the prophet in Satan's domain. This means that our natural decisions have spiritual implications. This is why spiritual intelligence is important, even though most believers highlight and promote cognitive intelligence, while others promote emotional intelligence.

How do we fit cognitive intelligence into spiritual dynamics? Let's take our experiences, for example. A wasted experience is one that has no conclusion backing it. This means that it is a season that has yet to end. Even though the traumas, the events and the people from that era of your life may be long gone, if you don't extract the proper conclusion from that particular season, it could only mean that you're still in it. This is why it is so easy for some people to manipulate their way back into your life. If you never leave the area code of a set of principles, you will remain under that principality, and the information that will be available to you will be the same information that you've been eating and regurgitating. What did you learn from the breakup? What about the fight you had with your friends? What I've learned is that we all desire better results and healthier relationships, but the problem is that not many of us extract the revelation from our failed or expired relationships. We just find some way to cast ourselves as victims, and then we use our good intentions and our victim status to lure in new friends and new lovers. This means that not many of us grow cognitively, and this can delay our growth spiritually. I immediately think about some of the people I've come across on my journey. I can't tell you how many times I've met anointed, God-fearing men and women who were, for lack of a better word, stuck. They were going in cycles and circles because they'd gotten stuck in the seasons they were in. As I journeyed through those seasons, I had the privilege and the pleasure of meeting these souls, and like most people, I was distracted by their potential. I saw where God wanted to take them and I thought they were moving forward because of their levels of mastery. Over time, I had to come face-to-face with the truth when my time in those seasons began to come to an end. You see, they'd mastered the seasons they were in, meaning they'd become some of the principle-setters or master manipulators of those seasons, but they were stuck. They loved being the teachers of the seasons they were in, so much so that they refused to become students in the seasons that awaited them. I've literally witnessed people turning from the faith to embrace other deities, and for what? Because they wanted the Most High God to serve them! They wanted something inside His will, but they didn't want to go through the process to get it. They refused to learn from their natural experiences and their spiritual encounters. The spirit realm attempted to reach them by allowing them to experience the same events with different people, but their ears and eyes weren't open, and talking to them about their issues was like talking to the walls of a cave. Sure, you can hear your voice echoing over and over again, but it didn't move them at all. They wanted what they wanted, when they wanted it, and if God wasn't going to give it to them, they'd elected to find themselves other gods. To be honest with you, it is super surreal to watch a person who's proudly proclaimed Jesus as their Lord and Savior suddenly turn around and renounce Him. This is because they placed their cognitive intelligence over their spiritual intelligence.

Do you want to build Godly relationships that stand the

test of time and flourish in every season? If so, follow the steps below:

1. Give God your heart and don't take it back.
2. Heal. Hurt people not only hurt people, but they also attract hurt people.
3. Exalt spiritual intelligence over cognitive and emotional intelligence. Don't try to look and sound smart; wisdom is the principle thing.
4. Keep moving forward. Never allow your concept of loyalty to lock you into a season that God has graced you to come out of.
5. Give God His place in every area of your life. Let Him reign as Lord in every dimension of your heart.

SUBMITTING TO THE TRUTH

Submission. This word alone could start wars and rumors of wars. This is because submission requires you to acknowledge someone as your superior, and then you have to follow that person's lead. This sounds safe enough if you've had great leaders, starting with your parents, but if the authority figures in your life have failed you, led you astray, traumatized you or just ruined their own lives, the concept of submission may seem scary or offensive to you. But what if I told you that we are ALL submitting to something or someone? It's true. We naturally submit to what we believe. Let's look at the definition of "submission" before we go any further. Oxford Languages defines the word "submit" as:

- accept or yield to a superior force or to the authority or will of another person.
- subject to a particular process, treatment, or condition.

When most people hear the word "submit," they think that you're telling them to allow another human being to control them, and the minute you let that word escape your mouth, they immediately start having flashbacks of the authority figures who've mismanaged them. This is why they have such negative and explosive responses. For example, a woman who's been raped and abused by her father would start thinking about being under the tutelage and authority of another male who's like her father. The sad part is—she may have never seen true, healthy and Godly authority or submission modeled in front of her. All the same, submission is a part of the honor culture. Within the walls of this culture, you will find order; this includes the systems of hierarchy and protocol, and you have to respond to every chain of command the right way. Where there is no order, there will be disorder (also known as chaos); these are the states in which people who hate honor and order live. This is why I referred to the aforementioned woman's situation as sad; she may subject herself to a lifetime of mediocrity because of the evils her father has done to her. In other words, her villain would win while she, yet again, paid the price. Victimhood is a neighborhood of thinking that we should all break out of. This is why leaders are important. Unfortunately, a lot of people who are raised by demonized people don't cross over into the realm of honor because they genuinely fear submission and authority figures.

Let's look at a few scriptures that talk about submission. Note: the following scriptures were taken from the ESV Bible.

- **Romans 13:1-7:** Let every person be subject to the governing authorities. For there is no authority except from God, and those that exist have been instituted by God. Therefore whoever resists the authorities resists what God has appointed, and those who resist will incur judgment. For rulers are not a terror to good conduct, but to bad. Would you have no fear of the one who is in authority? Then do what is good, and you will receive his approval, for he is God's servant for your good. But if you do wrong, be afraid, for he does not bear the sword in vain. For he is the servant of God, an avenger who carries out God's wrath on the wrongdoer. Therefore one must be in subjection, not only to avoid God's wrath but also for the sake of conscience.

- **1 Peter 5:5**: Likewise, you who are younger, be subject to the elders. Clothe yourselves, all of you, with humility toward one another, for "God opposes the proud but gives grace to the humble."
- **Hebrews 13:7**: Obey your leaders and submit to them, for they are keeping watch over your souls, as those who will have to give an account. Let them do this with joy and not with groaning, for that would be of no advantage to you.
- **Ephesians 5:22–33**: Wives, submit to your own husbands, as to the Lord. For the husband is the head of the wife even as Christ is the head of the church, his body, and is himself its Savior. Now as the church submits to Christ, so also wives should submit in everything to their husbands. Husbands, love your wives, as Christ loved the church and gave himself up for her, that he might sanctify her, having cleansed her by the washing of water with the word,
- **Titus 3:1-2**: Remind them to be submissive to rulers and authorities, to be obedient, to be ready for every good work, to speak evil of no one, to avoid quarreling, to be gentle, and to show perfect courtesy toward all people.

How did something God commanded us to do become such a hated event? This is because most people don't understand what submission is, and many religions have passed off fear, abuse and control as submission. True submission can never be separated from the truth. What does this mean? Again, we are all submitting to something or someone. We submit to whatever or whomever it is that we trust, but get this, submission isn't just doing what someone says. Oftentimes, it is following the lead of another person; it means to pattern yourself after someone. Jesus said in John 5:19, "Truly, truly, I say to you, the Son can do nothing of his own accord, but only what he sees the Father doing. For whatever the Father does, that the Son does likewise." Let me explain it this way—you will always trust and submit to the truth regarding another human being (as we discussed in Relational Acuity 3.0). For example, Haley is married to Connor, and both Haley and her husband are devout Christians with ministerial titles. However, Haley does not trust her husband, and because she doesn't trust him, she won't submit to him. Better yet, she does trust her husband, but not in a good way. You see, Connor has been gambling since before he'd met his wife, and after going to rehab a few times, he'd just had another relapse. Notice in Ephesians 5:33, Apostle Paul says, "Nevertheless let every one of you in particular so love his wife even as himself; and the wife see that she reverence her husband." Husbands were instructed to love their wives, while wives were instructed to reverence or respect their husbands. The truth is, you cannot respect someone you do not trust or, better yet, if your trust points away from what they're saying. So, if your husband says he's going to go right, you expect him to go left, or if your wife tells you that she prefers the light on when she rests, but you believe that she truly prefers the lights to be off. Trust is built on your history with a person, and you will trust what the individual repeatedly shows or demonstrates to you. So, while Connor has been demanding that his wife trust him, the fact is that she trusts that he will go and gamble away their money; this is the truth that she's submitted to. Therefore, she has trouble submitting to what her husband says; instead, she submits to what he has repeatedly done. Let me explain it this way. In the realm of the spirit, there are two kingdoms; they are:

- Kingdom of God.
- Kingdom of Darkness.

Each kingdom has a temperature. The temperature of God's Kingdom is good or righteousness; the temperature of the demonic kingdom (kingdom of darkness) is bad or evil. The kingdom of man is the bridge between both kingdoms, and while those kingdoms cannot be reconciled, they communicate or express themselves through the kingdom of man. Connor has an account in both kingdoms and the accent of both kingdoms, and because he and his wife are one (biblically speaking), his wife has access to both of his accounts. She also knows both of his accents. In the kingdom of darkness, Connor has built a lot of trust with the devil. What do I mean by this? Simply put, Satan trusts Connor to gamble away his money. He knows how and when to seduce Haley's husband. Connor also has an account in the Kingdom of God; this account is a trust–

fund of sorts called faith. This particular account is in the negative. Therefore, Haley has to withdraw from the account that has a surplus, and that account happens to be Connor's ungodly habit. When Connor throws a tantrum and demands that his wife trusts him, she almost always throws a tantrum of her own because the only trust she can extend to her husband is in the fact that he will gamble away their money. Do you now see how trust and submission work? A person will always draw from the accounts that they've had with you; this is their history with you. Sure, we can give people an advancement on our trust, but this advancement has to be repaid by the individual over time; this repayment comes in the form of the individual proving himself or herself to be trustworthy. Of course, this trust is established in the seasons of testing and temptation. If the individual aces all of his or her tests, we will extend more trust to the individual, meaning we'll give the person in question a measure of grace that he or she has not earned. Whenever our trust is betrayed, we respond through an event called distrust. What this means is the person's trust-fund goes in the negative and the balance is transferred to the kingdom of darkness. We then trust that the person will betray, disappoint and hurt us more than we trust what the person says.

I'm no fan of counseling couples, so anytime someone attempts to book me for marriage counseling, I refer that person to someone else. For one, I don't want to be blamed for the destruction and failure of someone's relationship should that person take my advice, thus provoking a not-so-quiet storm in their marriage. The truth is that the only way a problem can and will be eradicated is if one or both of the spouses learns to communicate, not just their problems with the other spouse, but to communicate a satisfactory solution. All the same, boundaries have to be set and enforced, and as a leader, I have to communicate this with the person who feels slighted. For example, I might have to say something like, "You have to let him know that coming home in the middle of the night is not okay" or "You have to blatantly tell her that her father cannot move in with the two of you." Believe it or not, these are sound instructions, but when enforced, they can provoke the other spouse to walk away from his or her marriage. Whenever you give this type of advice to a married person, you have to be fully aware of just how your advice may positively or negatively impact that person's marriage. You also have to be aware of the fact that people can and will blame you for the destruction or the condition of their marriages. For example, Haley may repeatedly come to you complaining about Connor's gambling problem, and one day, you may say to her, "Hey, you've spoken with him. You two have gone to counseling, and he has fired or rejected every therapist I've sent his way. He's gone to rehab, but he quit going after three days. At this point, you have to realize that he's going to continue gambling with or without you. This issue is rooted deeper than his love for you and his love for himself; it is even rooted deeper than his love for God. At this point, you have to understand that challenging him is not going to do anything but start another argument. All the same, your children are in that negative and toxic environment.

They see you weeping and they see the two of you arguing, so they'll likely need a lot of therapy as they grow older. Now, you have to consider this fact and use it to make a decision. Again, the fact is, he's not going to stop gambling anytime soon. In truth, he may never stop gambling. Now, you have to ask yourself this question— 'Can I live with a gambler for the rest of my life? What would that look like?' Then again, ask yourself this—'Am I willing to live without Connor? What would that look like?' You also may want to consider individual counseling, as opposed to marital counseling, after all, you have to start working on yourself; this is what will allow you to make a sound, sober and informed decision." In this, you are giving Haley sound advice. At this point, she has to count the costs since she didn't do this before marrying Connor. Now, she has to divorce her beliefs about Connor and marry the truth; her husband is a gambler. Can he be changed? Yes. Should she remain with him? That's her decision. She has to determine whether or not she can remain married to him in the state that he's in. Let's say that Haley goes home and does the homework you've given her. She takes a few days to ask herself if she could live with her husband in the state that he's in. She also stops tracking his movements and arguing with him as you advised. After four days, Haley reaches out to you to say, "Hey, I've made my mind up. I have to divorce Connor. I can't subject my children to this for the rest of their childhood." You don't encourage her to leave, nor do you encourage her to stay. As a counselor or coach, your job is to remain neutral; that is unless someone's life is in danger. Three days later, you discover that Haley has deleted you from her Facebook page. Surprised, you navigate to her page to see what turn of events has taken place. She's updated her photo to a picture of her and Connor, and her latest Facebook post reads, "What God has brought together, let no man put asunder. I'll fight for 'us' for the rest of my life!" Being the professional you are, you decide to not call and question Haley, after all, she's an adult. She can do whatsoever she pleases, and you don't have to deal with the consequences of her choices. Nevertheless, Haley owes you $376 for her last few sessions, so you send her an invoice. This prompts her to email you. The email reads, "Hey, I'm sorry things had to end this way, but in no way, shape, form or fashion could I allow you to keep counseling me when you are against my marriage. You said it yourself—don't give value to people who don't value what you value. I took your advice and I am discontinuing my services with you. As for the bill, I don't feel like I should have to pay it, so please consider clearing my balance because your advice almost destroyed my marriage. I hope that this email finds you well. God bless you!" This is crazy, right? It's exactly what active leaders go through at least once a week! What happened here? How did Haley go from complaining about her husband to casting you in her story as the villain? Believe it or not, every good story has a villain, and the villain typically loses in the end. Haley doesn't want to lose her husband, so she had to find another villain, but to do this, she also had to tell herself a lie that's even more distracting than the lies her husband has been telling her. She told herself that, while Connor was gambling away their livelihood, you were a bitter woman or a lustful man who'd stop at nothing to see her and Connor broken up. She fantasized about Connor standing on a stage in front of a medium-sized to a large audience someday; he'd be successful, free of his demons, and more than anything, he'd be incredibly appreciative of her. In her fantasy, Connor stood on a stage looking remarkably handsome and her now sober husband asked her to stand up before saying to the audience, "Do you see that woman right there?!" His hilarious but brilliant speech would now be interrupted by a serious and passionate tone as he looked at the woman sitting in the front row. "She is the epitome of a Proverbs 31 woman! She stayed with me when everyone around me walked away. She even had a counselor tell her to leave me, but she stuck it out! She got talked about, laughed at, and repeatedly rejected because of me, and yet, she stayed." His speech would be interrupted by a masculine hiccup, followed by a well of tears. Nevertheless, this would prove that, while he is masculine and strong, his wife happens to be his soft spot. "This is why I love her so much, and no raggedy woman on this planet can ever take her place!" Connor would then blow a kiss at his wife. The audience would then clap as Haley softly patted away her tears with a silk handkerchief (customized, of course). This fantasy was her drug of choice, and while it rendered her a temporary high, it allowed her to escape her reality if but for a moment. Casting you as a villain against "them" helped her to create a narrative that would encourage her and Connor to stand on the same side of a battlefield once again. In this, she has submitted to a lie because she did not want to face the truth. I'm sharing this to say that, while people can and do submit to the truth regarding other people, there are times when people create their own versions of the truth. We call this state of mind "denial."

Every person in your circle is submitting to a fact, a truth, a suspicion or a blatant lie about you. This is why it is dangerous to place a comma where God has placed a period. What does this mean? In short, a person's limited view of you will always tell you how far that person can walk with you. The end of every season is marked by a period, but this period isn't just a dot randomly placed on a sheet of paper or a word document. It is a space of time when the truth regarding a person is revealed. This period took place, for example, when Haley discovered that her husband had relapsed and returned to his old ways. This isn't to say that she should have divorced or left him; this is to say that before she continued building with him, she needed to honor the period behind the sentence she'd served with him. In other words, she needed to start her journey with him as a sober woman, but to do this, she would have to write herself a clean bill of health called the truth. This is what the Bible refers to as the proverbial "way of escape." By doing this, she could truly tally up the costs of what it would mean to remain married to him, and then she could soberly decide if she could afford to pay those fees or if she wanted to pay those fees. Would remaining married to him cost Haley her sanity, or would it eventually cost her the respect of her children? What about her house? Would she lose it to foreclosure as Connor's gambling problem ate away at their finances? What about their children's tuition? What about their reputation? This is what it means to count the costs. Get this—if she continues lying to and love-bombing herself about her husband, Haley will likely enter the realm of witchcraft. How so? Because she'll keep arguing, punishing and trying to force her husband to be the man that she's imagined him to be. This is behavioral modification, not heart transformation. He can only be changed or transformed by the renewing of his mind and, of course, the Word of God is the only true way to transform a mind. Everything else falls under the categories of manipulation and control. For example, while rehab is great and necessary, it deals more with behavioral modification; this is oftentimes instigated through confession, therapy and accountability. And yes, every addict should go to rehab! However, have you ever noticed that behaviorists and psychologists promote the belief that once an alcoholic, drug addict or a gambler always an alcoholic, drug addict or gambler? Do you understand why this is? It's simple. They know how to address the behaviors, but as long as that person's heart is not healed and those demons are not cast out, they are likely to return to their addictions. Another way of saying this is—if their voids are not addressed, they will return to the destructive patterns that once jarred their lives. You can keep building with whomsoever you want to build with. Just know that wherever God places a period, you have to meet Him in that space; that's the space of revelation and decision. It's where you'll have your encounter with the truth, and get this—after hearing and understanding the truth about her husband and what their relationship will look like, Haley can freely continue her relationship with him, but she'll have to remain prayerful, refrain from trying to control her husband, get regular bouts of both deliverance and counseling, and she'll have to obey the Lord as it relates to her husband. Does this mean that he will change his ways? Nope. This is why the Bible said, "But if the unbelieving depart, let him depart. A brother or a sister is not under bondage in such cases: but God hath called us to peace" (1 Corinthians 7:15). Understand this—by obeying the Word, Haley will intentionally or unintentionally instigate James 4:7, which reads, "Submit yourselves therefore to God. Resist the devil, and he will flee from you." This is why the scriptures said to "let" the unbeliever leave if he or she wants to leave, after all, the fight is a spiritual one, not a natural one.

Getting back to the topic at hand, it is important that you always pursue the truth rather than pursuing what makes you feel comfortable or what makes you feel giddy. When you discover the truth, submit to it because the truth is sometimes a period; it is your meeting space with God. Honor that space! Don't reject it and refuse to move forward, otherwise, you'll go back and live in the past mentally and emotionally while your body lives in the present. This disconnect between your soul and your body will ultimately lead to you making a lot of unwise and detrimental decisions that could potentially cost you your future.

RELATIONAL DYNAMICS

Common questions that I get include:
1. My family isn't saved, nor do they want to be saved. Should I disconnect from them?
2. There are people on the leadership team at my church who are not living for the Lord. Should I go and find a new church?
3. Ever since I've gotten saved, I've been wrestling with whether or not I should disconnect from my unsaved friends or not. What do you advise?
4. My friends are saved! As a matter of fact, I met them at church and they've been saved longer than I have, but they are not Godly. I'm confused. They pray, they prophesy and they even serve at church, but outside of church, they are not living for the Lord. What should I do?

Relational dynamics can be complex to the new believer as well as seasoned believers who want to grow in their relationships with God. Righteousness is like a pyramid; it has a bottom which is broad and a top that is narrow. Most people reside in the common area; this is the bottom of that pyramid, and the higher you go up that mountain, the less people you will find in your circle. As a matter of fact, the more you grow in the Lord, the more intentional you'll become whenever you are building new relationships or sustaining others. Howbeit, before I go any further into this lesson, let me say this—holiness is NOT a function, it is faith at work, and this faith manifests or materializes in the way that we function. Why is this important? Because a lot of believers are immature and religious, and by religious, I mean that they are works-minded. They attribute holiness to appearances, functions, titles and rituals, not realizing that holiness is a heart condition. It means to have the heart of God. "Because it is written, Be ye holy; for I am holy" (1 Peter 1:16).

Most families are connected by sin. As a matter of fact, if you are a believer who genuinely and wholeheartedly loves the Lord, and you've given your life for the gospel, meaning you're intentional about living holy, one thing you'll notice is this—you'll be shut out and shunned by a lot of professing believers. This is because the agreements that link most people together are carnal in nature. Sure, believers affiliate and associate themselves with other believers because, quite frankly, we all want people around us who are like-minded, however, the dominant conversation for those believers is often fueled by sin. The reason for this is—Satan, somehow, managed to convince several generations of believers and non-believers that any and everything that's good, Godly and spiritual is boring because it has to be approached in seriousness, but the carnal matters or desires of the heart, because they are not sacred, are free-range fun. And who wants to befriend or walk closely with someone who is always uptight or boring? Howbeit, the truth of the matter is, while God is sacred, His Kingdom is sacred and the Word is sacred, holiness is not boring; it is simply acknowledging that you, along with the rest of God's children, are set apart from the world (sacred). Please note that the Greek word for "sacred" is "hieros," and according to Strong's Concordance, it means "holy; set apart." To understand what it means to be set apart, let's go to the scriptures.

- **Matthew 13:24-30 (ESV):** He put another parable before them, saying, "The kingdom of heaven may be compared to a man who sowed good seed in his field, but while his men were sleeping, his enemy came and sowed weeds among the wheat and went away. So when the plants came up and bore grain, then the weeds appeared also. And the servants of the master of the house came and said to him, 'Master, did you not sow good seed in your field? How then does it have weeds?' He said to them, 'An enemy has done this.' So the servants said to him, 'Then do you want us to go and gather them?' But he said, 'No, lest in gathering the weeds you root up the wheat along with them. Let both grow together until the harvest, and at harvest time I will tell the reapers, "Gather the weeds first and bind them in bundles to be burned, but gather the wheat into my barn."'"

- **Matthew 13:36-43 (ESV):** Then he left the crowds and went into the house. And his disciples came to him, saying, "Explain to us the parable of the weeds of the field." He answered, "The one who sows the good seed is the Son of Man. The field is the world, and the good seed is the sons of the kingdom. The weeds are the sons of the evil one, and the enemy who sowed them is the devil. The harvest is the end of the age, and the reapers are angels. Just as the weeds are gathered and burned with fire, so will it be at the end of the age. The Son of Man will send his angels, and they will gather out of his kingdom all causes of sin and all law-breakers, and throw them into the fiery furnace. In that place there will be weeping and gnashing of teeth. Then the righteous will shine like the sun in the kingdom of their Father. He who has ears, let him hear.

What did the angels do? They set God's people (wheat) apart from Satan's children (tares). Amazingly enough, we've come to believe that this particular parable speaks of the rapture, and it is then that the reapers (angels) will come and separate the wheat from the tares, but the aforementioned parable is not talking about a futuristic event. The weeds and the tares have already been separated in the realm of the spirit, even though we walk closely together in the Earth's realm. This is why God said, "By their fruits, you will know them."

In the aforementioned scriptural passage, we read about the wheat and the tares (see Matthew 13:24-30). Please note that the modern-day name for "tare" is "lolium temulentum," also known as darnel rye.
Check out this article from Wikipedia:

"Darnel usually grows in the same production zones as wheat and was a serious weed of cultivation until modern sorting machinery enabled darnel seeds to be separated efficiently from seed wheat. The similarity between these two plants is so great that in some regions, darnel is referred to as "false wheat". It bears a close resemblance to wheat until

the ear appears. The spikes of L. temulentum are more slender than those of wheat. The spikelets are oriented edgeways to the rachis and have only a single glume, while those of wheat are oriented with the flat side to the rachis and have two glumes. Wheat will appear brown when ripe, whereas darnel is black. Darnel can be infected by an endophytic fungus of the genus Neotyphodium and the endophyte-produced, insecticidal loline alkaloids were first isolated from this plant.
The French word for darnel is ivraie (from Latin ebriacus, intoxicated), which expresses the drunken nausea from eating the infected plant, which can be fatal. The French name echoes the scientific name, Latin temulentus "drunk" (Source: Wikipedia/Lolium temulentum).

How do you distinguish false wheat (darnel) from true wheat? Examine the ear. In Matthew 11:15, Jesus said it this way, "He that hath ears to hear, let him hear." This is important because a lot of believers endure unnecessary warfare because they don't understand spiritual principles. Of course, these principles are outlined for us in the Bible, but a lot of people don't read their Bibles. I can't tell you how many times I've come across men and women who are "under attack" because they kept trying to open deaf ears, not realizing that the war is not against flesh and blood, but against powers, principalities, the rulers of this dark world and spiritual wickedness in high places (Ephesians 6:12). What does all of this mean? It means that you should approach every relationship and conversation the way the

Bible tells you to approach them. Matthew 7:6 reads, "Give
not that which is holy unto the dogs, neither cast ye your
pearls before swine, lest they trample them under their
feet, and turn again and rend you." The word "dogs" is
used to symbolize unbelievers, while the word "swine" is
used in conjunction with demonized people. Do you see
what the Bible says will happen if you give wisdom to
unbelievers who don't want that wisdom or to demonized
people? The Bible says they'll trample that information,
meaning, they will devalue and demean it, but that's not
all! They will then turn around and rend you. The word
"rend" here means attack. I've failed this test many times.
I've attempted to have Godly, wisdom-filled, spiritual
conversations with loved ones, hoping that it would open
their eyes and they would turn to Christ. Boy, was I wrong!
Instead, I've listened quietly (in regret, might I add) as my
words were twisted, my character was assassinated and
my motives were questioned. I sat there quietly, reminding
myself of what God said in His Word, all the while allowing
the verbal backlash to serve as a lesson to me. I'd spoken
into deaf ears. "Love you too," I'd say as I hung up the
line, knowing that the individual in question would not be
speaking to me for yet another year or two. Like many
believers, I've wrestled with the question—how do you have
a relationship with an unsaved person who clearly doesn't
want God unless God agrees to serve that person? I say
this because a lot of our family members do believe in God;
they believe that Jesus is Lord, but they are not serving
the Lord, nor do they desire to serve Him. In truth, some
of them are mad at Him or frustrated with the idea of
giving up their sinful lifestyles to follow Him. So, they'll

(occasionally) go to church; they'll even respect the house of the Lord (to an extent), but they will not and do not submit themselves to Him in any way, shape, form or fashion. What should you do if the majority of your family is like this? Remember that we are multidimensional creatures. This means that each person in your family is multifaceted or, better yet, that person has many faces. The same is true for you. Ungodly and/or unsaved people are masterful at finding your dark face. Your dark face is the side of you that lacks wisdom and, is therefore, filled with voids. They'll keep spinning you around or twisting the conversation until they find that particular face of yours, and that's the face that they'll speak with. It's the face that they will look for every time you come around. Your objective is to show them your good faces; these are the areas of you that are Godly, mature and producing good fruits. What should you do with your dark faces?

1. Plant them in the Bible until the light comes on.
2. Show them to your pastors, counselors and mentors so you can get help. (Note: I don't mean you should act out; I mean you should expose these faces by telling your wise counselors your fears, habits, evil thoughts and desires).
3. Put a wall in front of them. Another word for this wall is "boundary." This means that if someone tries to spin you around, the first line of defense is to refuse to be turned. You do this by shifting the conversation to one of your good or God-faces. If the person manages to spin you around, let that person come in contact with a wall. Again, this is called stonewalling. What this looks like is—you

remaining silent, not answering their questions and not allowing them to trigger an ungodly response.

4. Remove yourself from the situation. You should excuse yourself from that person's presence if the individual is overly determined to see the worst in you. This makes me think of the year 2009. I was married at the time, and the man I was married to (we'll call him Rodger) was in Mississippi with me. We were living at my mother's house temporarily after having moved to the States from Germany. It was a Sunday afternoon, and I'd just returned from church. I was excited because we'd had such an amazing and powerful time in the Lord, and I wanted to tell my family about it. No one had come to church with me that day (as usual). I was a babe in Christ at that time, so I was somewhat religious. My mother was blasting the Blues, and the song she was playing was incredibly ungodly. I got frustrated and reminded her that it was Sunday. "Why are you playing this kind of music on a Sunday?" I asked. My mother found my response funny, and so did Rodger. Before long, they thought it would be a good idea to start taunting me. My mother turned around and started grinding on me while the music played. Meanwhile, Rodger got behind me and held my arms, pinning them over my head so I couldn't move. Getting a standing lap dance from my mother was not a highlight reel moment, especially given the fact that they were mocking me. Again, they were playing, but that event was too much for me at that moment. Being pinned or held in any way

triggered anger in me; this is likely because I'd just escaped an abusive relationship before meeting and marrying Rodger. Obviously, I hadn't healed before jumping in another relationship. I don't remember how I broke Rodger's grip, but what I do remember was that I wasn't gentle at all in that moment. Violence. I felt violent because I felt violated. I raised my voice and screamed at everyone. I then stormed out of the house and went for a long walk. Did I behave properly? No. Sure, it was good that I left that situation, but I let it go too far before I decided to leave. They wanted to see the Tiffany I'd become, not the one I was becoming. In this, they'd twirled me around until they found a dark face. When they did, I behaved like an animal, but I quickly recovered and left while they remained in the house laughing. Never allow people to bring out the worst in you. When God gives you a way of escape, use it.

False wheat doesn't have ears once it's matured. In this, I could not say that my mother or Rodger were false wheat because they hadn't matured yet. What I had to learn, however, was to guard every dimension of myself that was not mature, healed or Godly whenever engaging with them. Obviously, being married to Rodger made this feat nearly impossible, but when dealing with impossible things, you have to be intentional. However, when dealing with "church folks," one of the ways to see if the person is truly of God or not of God is to pay attention to how they navigate conversations. Are they too prideful to hear anyone, or do they listen and apply wisdom? Are they teachable or correctable, or do they fashion themselves as victims whenever a conversation takes a left turn? You want to know the difference so that you won't place swine or ungodly folks in your intimate circle, after all, demonized people will not allow you to place them in your intellectual circle unless they don't see an immediate need to connect themselves to you intimately.

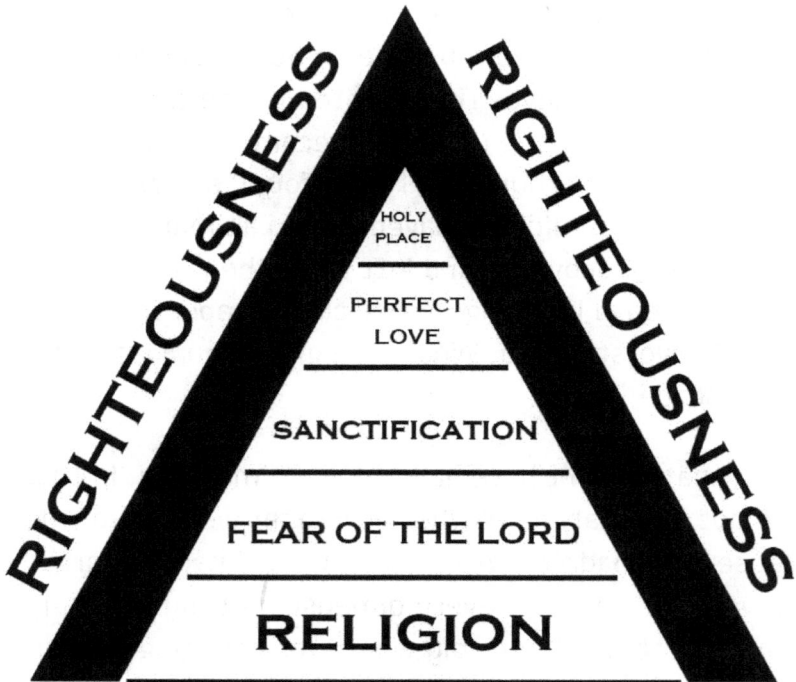

HOLY PLACE

PERFECT LOVE

SANCTIFICATION

FEAR OF THE LORD

RELIGION

RIGHTEOUSNESS RIGHTEOUSNESS

The above pyramid deals with relational dynamics or righteousness. When you first start your journey as a believer, you enter Zone 5. This is the bottom of the mountain or pyramid; this is the common area. It's where you'll find most believers, both new and seasoned. It's where you'll find backsliders and the like. It's where you'll find religious folks who have a form of Godliness but completely deny the power thereof. If you want to be accepted by the masses, you can never leave this area. If you are a slave to rejection, you cannot leave this area unless you fight your way through rejection's barbed wires. These barbed wires include ungodly soul ties, people-pleasing, fear of abandonment, fear of rejection, loneliness, unforgiveness, a need for affirmation and the worst of them all, religiousness. Religiousness, simply put, is the state of being arrested, bound and in agreement with the religious doctrines of man that promote fear, flesh (gender, race, titles) and twisted interpretations of the scriptures over God's Word. Religious people promote appearances over righteousness. To ascend the mountain of the Lord, you have to have a relationship with God outside of man's interpretation of who God is. In other words, God doesn't want you to have a third-party relationship with Him. He wants to talk to you face-to-face. Howbeit, we deny Him this right when we allow people to define Him for us, rather than us pursuing Him so that we can get to know Him intimately, after all, God wants to be the head of our intimate circles, just like He's invited us to sup with Him. When God sanctified us, He set us apart from others, but He didn't necessarily move us physically. What He did was give us access to information that others in our zones didn't have access to. This is wisdom and revelation from the planes or zones above us. In other words, He moved us dimensionally. Check out the next chart to see how this looks in the realm of the spirit.

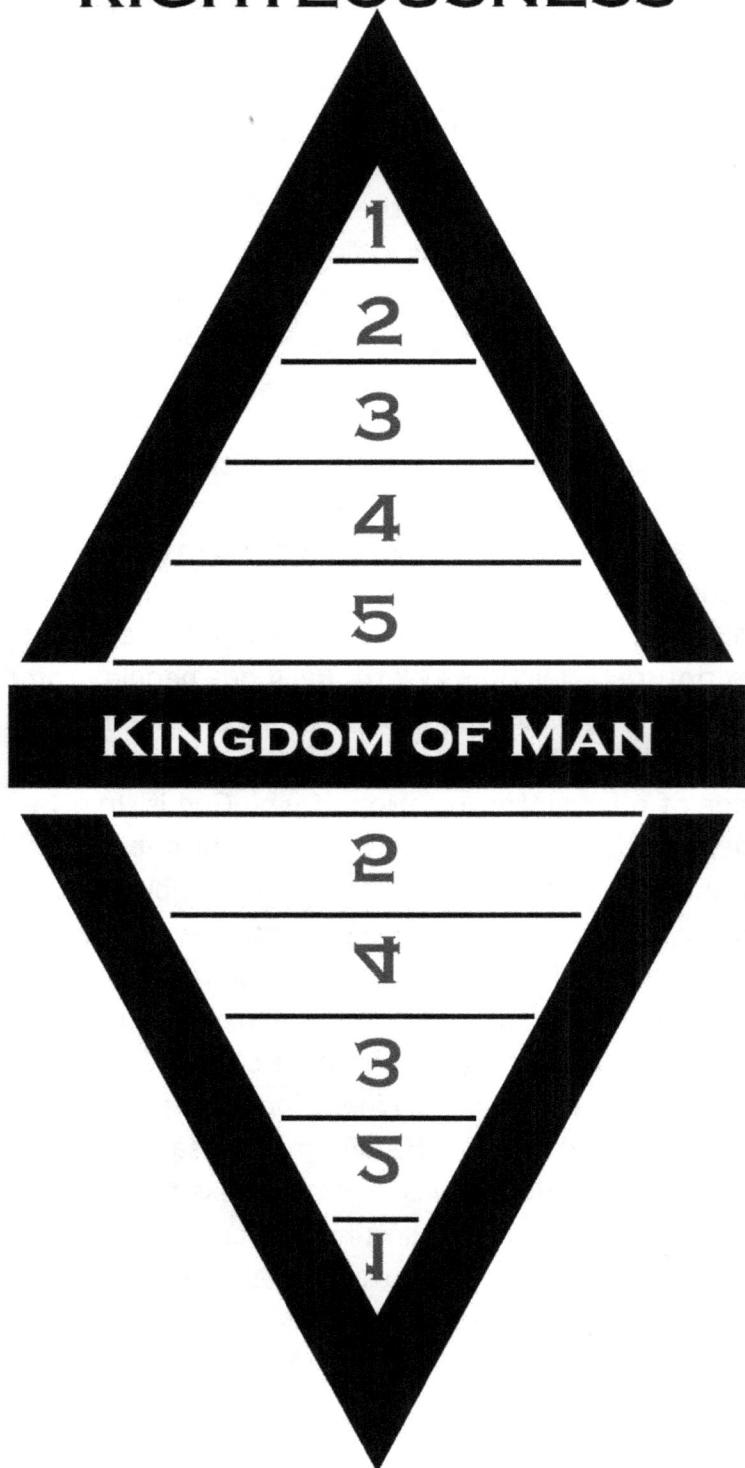

RIGHTEOUSNESS

:s

1
2
3
4
5

KINGDOM OF MAN

2
4
3
5
1

REBELLION

Notice in the drawing (see previous page) that there are two realms that we can move in; they are righteousness and rebellion or, better yet, we can move in the Kingdom of God or in the kingdom of darkness. We are already in the Kingdom of man, obviously. When we were unsaved, we were descending deeper into darkness. Remember when the Bible talks about the return of the unclean spirit, and how if that spirit returns, it will bring seven spirits more wicked than itself? By wicked, the Bible is referring to depth or debt. Understand that angels have varying ranks, so every fallen angel is not of the same rank. Some fallen angels ranked high in the Kingdom of God. To whom much is given, much is required. This means that their punishments will be greater because they had a greater level of responsibility. Another way of saying this is—they had more knowledge of God than the angels who were lower in rank. This means that they are lower on the pyramid or, better yet, they are more wicked than their evil demonic counterparts. Jude 1:6 reads, "And the angels which kept not their first estate, but left their own habitation, he hath reserved in everlasting chains under darkness unto the judgment of the great day." Therefore, the objective of Satan and his cohorts was and is to bring you into the kingdom of darkness and lead you further and deeper into the darkness, knowing that the more evil and rebellious you became, the more likely it was for God to cut the cords by turning you over to a reprobate mind. You see, the leash or line that held you to God is called mercy, but if you, after knowing Him, repeatedly take God's grace for granted, you are essentially denying Him.

Nevertheless, let's say that you got saved and you are now

in the common area; you are now in Zone 5. Please understand that the folks in Zone 5 are more relatable to you at that phase of your life. As a matter of fact, you'll be able to relate more to unsaved folks than you are to saved ones. All the same, if you keep focusing on the believers in Zone 5, you will either become like them or you'll descend into the darkness, reasoning within yourself that it is better to be sinful and aware of the state you're in than to be a fake Christian. As you ascend this mountain or pyramid in righteousness, you'll notice that a lot of your relationships will become strained, while others are severed altogether. This is because the soul ties that you have formed with some people won't be able to survive when you are several dimensions ahead or beneath another person. Keep in mind that the soul is comprised of the mind, will and emotions, so a soul tie isn't a tissue like structure that we can't see; it's the marrying of two perspectives, and the pastor that officiated that marriage is called a principle. This is why I don't chase people who put me on punishment simply because we didn't agree about something. Mature believers know how to have relationships with people that they don't wholeheartedly agree with because they understand that every disagreement is an opportunity to sharpen or be sharpened. If nothing else, it's definitely a learning experience.

As you ascend this pyramid, you will find that you are not able to relate with most people. For this reason, a lot of believers start their ascensions in Christ, and the moment they realize that their choices to follow Him closely would cost them many of their close and intimate relationships with friends and family members, they'd turned back because they didn't want to be that absent family member that the family talked about during family gatherings or that former friend who had been accused of betrayal. So, they descended back into Zone 5. This decision placed them outside of God's will and led them into the captivity of Jezebel. As discussed in Relational Acuity 2.0, whenever God grants you access to another dimension, if you don't ascend into that new space, you will find yourself locked in the old space, and you will become a principality or principle-setter in that space. This means that whenever people who are within your reach (mentally and spiritually) attempt to ascend past you, you will go out of your way to keep them from doing so. You'll find yourself saying (and believing) that holiness isn't necessary and Christians who attempt to live lives outside of righteousness are so heavenly-minded that they are no earthly good. You'll roll your eyes at people who truly want to embrace the heart of God, and you will be one of the giants they have to get past in order to ascend. This is not a good position to be in, after all, Goliath will eventually come in contact with David, and the young shepherd boy will use the Rock (Jesus) to defeat his enemy. All the same, getting locked in a dimension is called a stronghold, and a stronghold is a well-decorated comfort zone called denial, and denial is built on lies. I'm saying all of this to say—before you build a thing, count the costs! If you want to go to Zone 1 in Christ and maximize your full potential in Him, you have to understand that you'll be so dimensionally distant from a lot of people you once walked closely with that you will find yourself walking alone or with less than a handful of people. In truth, the journey up this pyramid is rather lonely. Each dimension is separated by a power veil; I call this veil shock or the shock treatment. Every time you go through the power veil, you will be shocked—shocked at who walks away from you, shocked at who betrays you, shocked at who continues to walk with you, shocked at who begins to walk with you! Over time, this electrical current won't affect you as much, as you'll come to grow used to seeing people fall away. Now, this isn't for the faint at heart or the people who just want to live underneath man's radar. This is for leaders and believers who want to be all they can be in Christ.

One of the things I'll challenge you to do is to look at your intimate and intelligence circles, and ask yourself the following questions:
1. What agreements or like interests connect me with (name each person in your circle)?
2. What deficiencies or strongholds connect me to (name each person in your circle)?
3. Is the dominant conversation with (name each person in your circle) carnal?

Let me address the elephant in the room. You do not have to sit around and talk about Jesus all day. However, it is important that conversations that are not Christ-centered are not laced with sin either. In other words, you don't want the tie or the agreement that links you with another person to be ungodly, otherwise, God may have to deliver you from that person or to the spirit in that person. Remember, whatever you feed grows and whatever you starve will die. I'm saying that to say this—it is possible to take what God has brought together and pervert it, and I'm not just talking about romantic relationships (even though they are included as well). It is possible (and relatively common) for people to take something good and season it with sin. Again, this is the product of how we view holiness versus carnality. All the same, it is possible to have a good and Godly connection that is not laced with sin to be fun. Remember that God created fun; Satan simply perverted our definition of fun. Know this—every conversation has algorithm attached to it. In layman's terms, every conversation continues until it is interrupted and assassinated by a contrary one. So, if you gossip with a person, the next time you see that person, they will affiliate you with gossip or whenever they have something ungodly to say, they'll think of you. I've come to realize that this is why there are so many prophets and prophetic people in caves (isolation) today. Many believers outside of the church truly want Godly connections with people, but they've experienced walking into church and witnessing a bunch of ungodly soul ties amongst the people and they were written off as "religious" or "too uptight" simply because they didn't want to drink, smoke, dance to ungodly music, have sex or engage in behaviors that are contrary to God's will. Feeling shunned and misunderstood, they began to self-isolate, watching church services online. This, to them, allowed them to get the Word and the revelation of the Word without having to deal with all of the toxic behaviors they've witnessed behind-the-scenes at their local assemblies. But, what if I told you that the runner or the one who self-isolates is outside of God's will? What if I told you that the ones behaving in an ungodly manner, all the while frequenting the church, were sin-sick believers who were in the right place at the right time? The church is the hospital for their souls! Don't get me wrong; God will and does address their behaviors, but one of the reasons that broken and ungodly people tend to overrun some churches is because a lot of the prophets and the prophetic people are off-post. Again, they are self-isolating, not realizing that they are the lights that these people need to see! Some would ask—what if the ungodly folks are the ones in leadership? What if the church has great pastors, but the people serving under those pastors are broken, toxic, messy, competitive and ungodly? What should we do then?! The answer is—show up and shine! Take your eyes off them and give God your undivided attention. Be a light in that place, understanding that darkness cannot stand in the presence of light. Over time, other people who are like yourself will come into the church and see your light; this will give them some company, and before long, the church will be overridden by the light (glory) and the presence of God! Do you see how this works? The enemy wants to drive you out of the church so that he can fill God's house with darkness; this divides the believers and makes us easier to defeat, after all, one can put a thousand to flight and two can put ten thousand to flight (see Deuteronomy 32:30).

What about family dynamics? Once again, the soul tie or link that connects most families together is sin. Notice that every time people gather with their families for holidays, weddings, funerals, baby showers, family reunions or other events, the dominant conversations are oftentimes ungodly. As Christians, we are encouraged to go to these events, remain connected with our families and just be a light in the midst of them, and while I don't disagree with the fact that we should be winning souls in our families, we have to always remind ourselves of this— the will of the human is sacred, so much so that even God doesn't infringe upon it. You see, when we gather together in church, we come together to worship the Lord, get an understanding of His Word and to fellowship with like-minded believers. This means that the overall objective (pinnacle) is Christ, regardless of the types of people and activities that we come in contact with while at church. Jesus said in John 12:32, "And I, if I be lifted up from the earth, I will draw all men unto me." You see, you can go to church and keep Christ as the center of your focus; you can join in during prayer, worship God, listen to the Word and the revelation, pay your tithes and then go home. If you try to connect with the people there, you will have to deal with the relational dynamics associated with each soul that you link yourself to. Now, I'm not discouraging you from building relationships, after all, in order for a church to be strong, we have to build relationships with one another. What I am encouraging you to do, however is:

1. **Test the spirit**. This requires that you not rush into calling someone your friend. Don't rush to give out your phone number. Watch people, pray about them and give out your contact information once you've seen them in several seasons of their walks with God. Also, test the spirit when you're talking to them. The goal is to see where they are on the

pyramid because if you're in Zone 2 and that person is in Zone 5, you can't necessarily form a friendship with that individual because you're too distant from one another dimensionally. You can, however, form a sisterhood or a mentor/mentee relationship with that person. Howbeit, if you form a friendship with the individual, you will ultimately get hurt. This doesn't mean that the other person is bad; it means that the individual may not be mature enough, healed enough or Godly enough to host the type of relationship you'll need to function properly in Christ. In other words, your relationship with that person will be dysfunctional and you will ultimately become the proverbial "strong friend" who has no one to turn to in times of distress.

2. **Use the right labels:** If the spirit in the person is ungodly or if the person is incredibly immature, place the person in your intellectual circle and place the correct label on that connection. For example, I may say to myself, "She's not healthy enough to be anyone's friend, but she's in the midst of a fight. That's my baby sister in Christ." In this, I have identified that the person in question is too young, spiritually speaking, to have a grown-up conversation or relationship with me. By identifying where she stands in Christ, I am able to host a Godly relationship with someone who may not be that Godly. Simply put, don't become best friends with a broken soul. Demonstrate the love of God to that individual and make sure that any conversation you have with that person is Christ-centered. In other

words, don't give place to slander, gossip or anything that's ungodly.

3. **Remember each label's allowances and limitations:** Going back to the previous example, let's say that I've decided Ramona is my baby sister in Christ. Even though Ramona may want to be closely connected with me, I've witnessed enough to know that such a connection could prove to be detrimental to what God wants to do in the church and in our personal lives. Each label should have allowances and restrictions, therefore, because I can see that Ramona is immature, I won't call her or answer any of her calls when I'm in a valley or a low place. Why is this? Because when we're hurting, we talk too much! I could easily end up handing her a burden that's too great or too heavy for her, and when you hand a heavy burden to a broken person, what's in that person will surface, whether the abundance of their heart is gossip or simply speaking word curses. This may also promote a trauma bond between Ramona and I, and these bonds are not easy to break. Lastly, it could establish a dark-faced connection between Ramona and I, whereas she'll never seek to see the good in me anymore. Instead, she'll always come looking for that broken side of me, even after I've healed and moved on, and this will undoubtedly cause our friendship to give up its ghost prematurely.

Going back to family dynamics, you have to consider the purpose or the nature of the family gathering before you decide whether or not to attend an event. For example, I don't celebrate Halloween, nor do I celebrate Easter, even though I do celebrate the resurrection of Christ. So, if my family did an Easter egg hunt, I wouldn't go, nor would I throw any money at the event. If they are gathering for a family reunion, I would have to draw from the history of my family before deciding if I'll be attending the event or what part of the event I'd consider attending. If the highlight of all of our family reunions is Uncle Earl bringing a new girlfriend while his wife crashes the event and assaults him, his new girlfriend and his nephew, I'm not going. If the highlight reel consists of cousin Patrick getting drunk and talking about how messed up our family is, while other family members mock and ask him a bunch of silly questions, I'm not going. If the highlight of that event is Uncle Junebug getting drunk and flirting with all of his nieces before groping Uncle Travis' wife, thus provoking a fight between Uncle Travis and himself, I'm not going. If the peak or grandest moment is the family sitting together and talking about how important it is for families to stick together before the table is nearly overturned by cousin Tammy simply because she's jealous of cousin Winnie's success, I'm not going. If the matriarch of the family brings us together to celebrate God and strengthen our connection as a family, I'll attend, even though I know that dysfunction will rear its ugly head at some point. The reason for this is—the dominant grace of a gathering is determined by the purpose and nature of that gathering. With that said, if I gathered with family while they came together to drink, dance and just be outright carnal, I could not be much of a light in that space because we are heading in different directions dimensionally. This is no different than me walking into a night club and holding up a sign that reads, "You're all going to hell if you don't give your life to Christ!" Not only would doing this repel people from God, the event would undoubtedly end in me being treated like a rag-doll and dragged across the dance floor by a group of angry, half-naked women. Again, Matthew 7:6 reads, "Give not that which is holy unto the dogs, neither cast ye your pearls before swine, lest they trample them under their feet, and turn again and rend you." Also consider what happened to Jesus when He went to His hometown. Mark 6:1-6 tells the story; it reads, "And he went out from thence, and came into his own country; and his disciples follow him. And when the sabbath day was come, he began to teach in the synagogue: and many hearing him were astonished, saying, From whence hath this man these things? and what wisdom is this which is given unto him, that even such mighty works are wrought by his hands? Is not this the carpenter, the son of Mary, the brother of James, and Joses, and of Juda, and Simon? and are not his sisters here with us? And they were offended at him. But Jesus said unto them, A prophet is not without honor, but in his own country, and among his own kin, and in his own house. And he could there do no mighty work, save that he laid his hands upon a few sick folk, and healed them. And he marveled because of their unbelief. And he went round about the villages, teaching." Don't get me wrong—I could potentially show up at some aspects of the reunion, but I'd avoid those events that typically bring out the worst in people.

Just be reminded of the following when dealing with relational dynamics:

1. Consider how high you want to go on the spiritual spectrum or pyramid, and then count the costs associated with the ascension. Are you willing to lose the relationships that are dearest to you? Are you okay with being misunderstood, persecuted and overlooked? How well do you deal with jealousy?

2. Consider where you are versus where the people in your circle are. Also consider where the people are who attempt to enter your circle; this way, you'll place them in the right circles and give them the proper labels.

3. Consider the overall point of your relationships. This is the pinnacle, peak or purpose of any given relationship. Also, remember that a peak can change if you get on a different mountain. Every conversation keeps you on a mountain or leads to another mountain. Don't allow the algorithm in your relationships to change simply because you had a conversation that you shouldn't have had, and if you ever find yourself slipping up and saying something you shouldn't have said, repent to God, apologize to that person, clean up what you said and commit to not returning to that conversation. Cast it away from you as word vomit. Don't reheat it and eat it again. Matthew 5:21-24 says it this way, "Ye have heard that it was said by them of old time, Thou shalt not kill; and whosoever shall kill shall be in danger of the judgment: But I say unto you, That whosoever is angry with his brother without a cause

shall be in danger of the judgment: and whosoever shall say to his brother, Raca, shall be in danger of the council: but whosoever shall say, Thou fool, shall be in danger of hell fire. Therefore if thou bring thy gift to the altar, and there rememberest that thy brother hath ought against thee; leave there thy gift before the altar, and go thy way; first be reconciled to thy brother, and then come and offer thy gift."

4. Pay attention to the temperature of your relationships. If the temperature goes from hot to cold, please know that a devil is somewhere lurking in your relationship, and it got in through gossip, slander, offense or by some ungodly means. This is why the Bible tells us to reconcile with one another before we attempt to present our gifts to God.

5. If you're at any event, familial or religious, and the focus shifts to something ungodly, leave that event! Let's say that you're at the family's reunion, and all is well; that is until cousin Pete showed up and started trying to bully the men at the reunion, your best out is to speak, in love, to cousin Pete. If he refuses to hear you or anyone else, and you notice that the whole family is now paying attention to cousin Pete and his antics, it is safer and wiser to leave that event than to watch all of your nephews beat cousin Pete to a pulp, only to have Pete go to his car and grab a pistol. While this may seem dramatic, this type of foolishness can and does happen!

6. Keep your dark faces turned to God. Every facet of

you needs time with God, of course, but don't allow people to pull on your dark side.

7. False wheat is poisonous. Don't eat from its table. Remember, you have to test the spirit, and this process takes time and intentionality! In other words, don't rush into anything with anyone. Good, healthy and Godly people won't run away or become offended when they notice that you're not running the speed limit towards their hearts, but unhealthy and ungodly folks will get mad when they can't access your heart as fast as they want to. This is because toxic people and narcissists are often in a hurry to extract whatever benefits they want from you, and any stop sign, yield sign or speed limit sign they see lets them know that pursuing you may end up being a waste of their time and a blow to their egos.

8. Don't give the folks in your intellectual circle the same benefits that the people in your intimate circle receive, otherwise, you'll end up with a one-sided relationship, whereas you'll become the giver/strong friend while the other party serves as the taker/victim. This creates a spiritual welfare system, whereas one party is receiving benefits, while the other party does all of the hard work. This sets the stage for entitlement in the taker (Consumer) and could land you in a very dark place with that person.

9. Don't cast your wisdom to earless people. If you notice that every time you talk about Jesus, business, education or anything positive, the person

you're communicating with either gets off the phone with you, repeatedly puts you on hold, tries to change the subject of the conversation or the person becomes offended, you have to stop talking with that person on that particular plane. You may have to stop talking to that person altogether. The best practice in a situation like this is to pay attention to the facet of you that the individual pulls on. Be sure to stonewall them in the areas that they are not healthy or Godly enough to access, or the areas that are ungodly, broken or in quarantine for now. Keep your conversations holy.

10. Stop trying to fit in with people before you mess around and succeed! God denies you access to some relationships because of the relational dynamics that will come into play should you build those relationships. Consider what we call "mean girl squads." These gatherings are nothing but mobile covens filled with beautiful bullies, both covert and overt. If you mess around and try to fit into a grouping like this, you will fall under the dynamics or principles of that group, whereas, there will be a group leader who will determine your role and function in that group. So, if she doesn't like the God-fearing, God-loving side of you, she will spin you around until she finds a dark side of you to highlight and showcase. Whenever your God-face shows up, she'll ignore or mistreat you. This taming process can go on for months or years until you finally start identifying yourself as the group clown, the security guard or whatever role you are given.

Authenticity = Authority

The prefix in both authenticity and authority is "aut." It comes from the prefix "auto," which means self.

- **Authentic** (Merriam Webster): not false or imitation: real; actual.
- **Authority** (Merriam Webster): power to influence or command thought, opinion, or behavior.

Let's create two characters; they are Tonya and Ashley. Both ladies are close friends, and while Ashley owns an up-and-coming mousse line, Tonya works as an administrative assistant for a popular attorney. All the same, Ashley is a single mother of one child and Tonya has three children that she's raising alone. The women have been friends for three years; they met when Ashley worked for the law firm that Tonya is currently employed at. However, Ashley started her own mousse line, and a year and a half after doing so, she was making enough money to fire her boss, so she quit the firm and started working for herself full time. Note: when Ashley first started her business, she nearly lost everything because she'd invested all of her savings into buying the products she needed to create her hair products, not to mention licensing, promotions and hiring two women to help her bring her vision to pass. Everyone, including Tonya, had once tried to encourage Ashley to close her business, citing that when the right time came, everything would come together, but Ashley did not take their advice. Instead, she continued to build her brand until it finally took off. While meeting with her employees one day, Ashley had gotten the bright idea to not only market her products on Instagram, but to also go into ten local hair salons within a 50 mile radius and offer the owners ten free cans of her product line in exchange for them allowing her to record their authentic reactions after using the mousse for the first time. She'd called around and found ten salons that agreed, and she went to four of those salons while her assistants went to three of those salons each. Every salon owner had the same reaction. They'd all found clients who would allow them to experiment on them with the product, and once they'd tried it, they stopped, read the back of the can and they'd all praised the product. The mousse's hold was like no other mousse on the market, and the scent of the mousse was beyond pleasant, plus, it didn't leave any residue. One salon owner said it smelled "clean," whatever that meant. In short, the mousse became a hit, and when Ashley posted all of the responses one day at a time, buying ads for each response, her business suddenly took off. Tonya was proud of her friend's success, and to be honest, she was a little envious of Ashley's newfound financial freedom. Ashley traveled from state to state and country to country promoting her product and vacationing along the way. She was living the dream life.

One day, Tonya calls Ashley to tell her the not-so-good news. "They fired me," Tonya said, referencing the law firm that she was once employed at. "They fired me because I was fifteen minutes late!" Ashley tries to comfort and encourage her friend, but Tonya is livid. "I'm not the only person who's been late at that firm!" she shouts. "Mrs. Singleton is late every Monday, but they don't say anything to her! They said I was late five times in two months, but I'm not the only one who isn't punctual!" Ashley lets her friend rant, and when she is done, Ashley says to her, "Tonya, this may be God's way of telling you to go into business for yourself. You've told me several times that you're tired of working for other people. Now is your chance to start that business you've been talking about for the last three years." Tonya excitedly agrees. "You're right! I didn't think about that! But which business idea should I start first? The clothing line or the jewelry line?" Ashley got into her car and let the call go to her car's Bluetooth before responding. "Whichever one God lays on your heart," she says. "You can start them both or, better yet, just do the research. Consider which opportunity requires the least investment and has the greatest profit margin and the least amount of red tape." After discussing Tonya's potential business for a few more minutes, the ladies got off the phone. Less than 48 hours later, Ashley received a text from Tonya that read:

> "Hey, Ash. I've been researching clothing and jewelry line startup, and both businesses require quite a bit of an investment, so I can't afford to launch them right now, but I've always wanted my own line of hair-care products, and after doing the research, I believe that I can pull it off if I start with one product at a time. I'm teetering between hair gel and mousse. I know you have your own mousse line. Which one would you recommend I get started with?"

Ashley is taken aback by the text. "I don't know if I should be offended, flattered or if I'm being a bad friend right now," Ashley says to herself aloud after she reads the text. "I don't want to be accused of gate-keeping information, but she needs to find what works for her. *(Sigh)*. This isn't going to end well." After thinking about it for a while, Ashley responds to Tonya via text. She says:

> "Hey there! Honestly, starting a hair-product business is pretty expensive. Remember, I lost everything when I first started. I sincerely recommend you do what you're most passionate about."

While Ashley was responding to her, Tonya was on Ashley's Instagram page scrolling through her feed. Over two thousand likes for an ad she'd posted a little over an hour ago? Tonya was sold. She wanted her own mousse line and she believed that Ashley was obligated, as a friend and a woman, to share everything she knew about starting and running a hair-care line. After scrolling through her feed, Tonya responds:

> "I completely understand, but a lot of the money you lost was due to trial and error, so it wouldn't be as expensive for me if I had you as my business coach. See? God works in mysterious ways! I think I've decided. I want to start off with mousse, but no worries, I won't compete with you because you're my friend. So, here are my questions:
>
> 1. Who created your logo and how much did he charge you? Can you send me his information?

2. I remember you once telling me that you buy your secret ingredient from a guy in China. Can you send me his info too, and how much does he charge you?

3. Who created your mockups? What about your website?

4. I'm thinking about calling my line Toni-Locs. What do you think of that?

Girl, I'm so excited about this! You should see me! I'm like a kid in a candy store right now!"

After receiving this particular text message, Ashley realizes that she has one of two choices. She could lose her friend by refusing to give her that information or she could lose her friend by giving her the info. Let me explain using a chart. In this chart, I want to show you what would happen either way. Be sure to read each section vertically to follow the stories.

Darned if She Does	Darned if She Doesn't
Ashley gives Tonya all of her resources.	Ashley points Tonya to a few books, videos and coaches that can help her start her journey.
Tonya gets a loan and uses that money to start her own hair-care line.	Tonya gets a loan and uses that money to start her own hair-care line.
Tonya decides against the name Toni-Locs and names her company Hair-Ash. This	Tonya decides against the name Toni-Locs and names her company Hair-Ash. This

Darned if She Does	Darned if She Doesn't
offends Ashley because her mousse is called Ash-Hold.	offends Ashley because her mousse is called Ash-Hold.
Tonya hires the same logo designer that Ashley worked with and has him to create a logo that looks remarkably similar to Ashley's logo.	Tonya has to find her own logo designer, and when she does, she has the designer to create a logo that looks remarkably similar to Ashley's logo.
Tonya puts a strain on the relationships between Ashley and her logo designer and Ashley and her manufacturer by demanding that they give her the same price that they gave Ashley.	Ashley's professional relationships with her logo designer and manufacturer are both safe, but her relationship with Tonya is now strained because she refused to share their information with Tonya.
Tonya begins marketing her new mousse line to the same audience that Ashley markets her product to.	Tonya begins marketing her new mousse line to the same audience that Ashley markets her product to.
Tonya's marketing ploys include passive-aggressively attacking Ashley's product online and attempting to sell her mousse 25 cents less than Ashley sells her mousse.	Tonya's marketing ploys include directly attacking Ashley's product online and attempting to sell her mousse at the same price point that Ashley sells her mousse.
Tonya becomes increasingly	Tonya becomes increasingly

Darned if She Does	Darned if She Doesn't
agitated with Ashley anytime Ashley promotes her product or does not abandon the marketing strategies that set her product apart from Tonya's.	agitated with Ashley anytime Ashley promotes her product or does not abandon the marketing strategies that set her product apart from Tonya's.
Tonya continues to ask for every resource, plan or strategy that Ashley has.	Tonya attempts to steal and sabotage every resource, plan and strategy Ashley has.
Tonya's business fails, while Ashley's continues to thrive.	Tonya's business fails, while Ashley's continues to thrive.
Tonya blames Ashley for the failure of her business.	Tonya blames Ashley for the failure of her business.
Tonya sells or gives away the information that Ashley freely gave her, thus making it more and more common.	Tonya can't sell or give away Ashley's contacts because Ashley didn't share them with her. So, she attempts to sell the info she acquired, but no one purchases it given the fact that her business failed.

Why did I create the above chart? I wanted to show that the journey would be somewhat different, but it would ultimately lead to the same conclusion. Ashley's mousse line was a product that belonged to her; it was likely her God-given idea. Howbeit, rather than finding her own path, Tonya decided to join Ashley on her journey, hoping to garner the same success that Ashley had attained. This is why it is difficult to form intimate relationships with people who have not found themselves. Who you authentically are is the person your blessings are attracted to. Your authenticity equals your authority. Howbeit, Tonya didn't understand this, so she put her friend in an awkward position. Don't get me wrong. Friends help friends; that's a given, and the problem wasn't centered around the fact that Tonya asked her friend for help. The real issue here is that she tried to gaslight her friend into giving up her ideas, rather than going on her own journey of self-discovery. She felt entitled to her friend's success, the product line she'd worked so hard to develop and her brand altogether. Understand this—anytime you tap into your authenticity, success will follow; the same is true for people who don't necessarily know who they are. This is because most people tend to think that success is a byproduct of being in the right place at the right time, so they will mimic whatever they see you finding success in. This doesn't necessarily make them bad; this is often the product of immaturity, hunger and a lack of identity.

Some people would argue that Ashley should be a team-player and give her friend, Tonya, all of the answers and resources she needs, but Matthew 7:6 (ESV) states, "Do not give dogs what is holy, and do not throw your pearls before pigs, lest they trample them underfoot and turn to attack you." When God gives you an idea, a strategy, a system or a method, that information is sacred. In short, don't give wisdom to people who don't have the capacity to host it or people who don't have enough history with God to appreciate it, otherwise, they'll take what you give them and they'll eventually turn around and attack you. Dogs, in the aforementioned biblical reference, represent unsaved people, whereas pigs are often symbolic of demonized people. Dogs also represent animalistic people or, better yet, folks who are led by their flesh. Tonya lacked both the discipline and the resources to start the types of businesses she wanted to start. We see the evidence of this in the fact that she wasn't disciplined enough to show up to work on time. People who make horrible employees often make even more horrible entrepreneurs because entrepreneurship requires an incredible amount of discipline and perseverance; it demands a great deal of self-sacrifice and focus. This means that it wasn't Tonya's season to launch those businesses or they weren't her businesses to start in the first place. She simply needed to pray and allow God to show her what her next move was, and God may have led her into the realm of entrepreneurship and started her with a light load, after all, He won't put more on us than we can manage. Think of it this way. If you walked into a gym for the first time and hired a personal trainer, that trainer would know not to give you a hundred-pound weight for starters. Your trainer would instead start you off with something manageable; from there, the trainer would gauge what you're able to lift comfortably. If you can lift 25 pounds without strain or struggle, the trainer may consider moving you up to a 50-pound weight. If the 50-pound weight is too heavy for you, the trainer will scale it back to 35 or 40 pounds, but get this, he won't let you stay there! For example, if your trainer decides that the 40-pound dumbbell is better suited for you, he will have you lift it for a couple of weeks, but after that, he will place a 50-pound weight in front of you. What is he doing? He's helping you to get stronger. All the same, he's helping you to increase your stamina. God does the same! With Tonya, God would have given her what she could manage, and by manage, I mean the amount of work and pressure that she could bear without coming out of character. If we saw a child carrying a box, and that child's knees were bent, we'd likely rush over and relieve the child of his or her burden. Why is this? Because we've determined that the load is too heavy for the kid. How did we take this determination? Simply put, we saw that the pressure caused the child to come out of his or her natural formation. The Bible compares us to clay and refers to God as our Potter (see Isaiah 64:8). The potter won't put too much pressure on the clay because doing so could deform it, so the potter puts just enough pressure on the clay to transform it into his vision. If the potter notices an impurity in the clay's mixture but somehow doesn't see it anymore, the potter wouldn't poke holes in the clay to find it. Instead, he'll put it on the potter's wheel and ever-so-gently place his hand on the clay as the wheel turns. This would cause each level or layer of the clay to conform to the potter's touch. Slowly, but surely the imperfection or impurity will surface, and when it does, the potter will scrape it off. We are the clay, and within us, there are impurities. God doesn't put an astronomical amount of pressure on us to get to those layers; instead, He puts the right amount of pressure on us, transforming us into the image in which He created us, and He deals with those impurities as they surface. Understand that some people will curse at you or even attempt to assault you if they are under too much pressure, and while we can discuss the fact that the anger, the blasphemous words and the violent tendencies are already in them, it is better for us to focus on this fact—God deals w th us in layers. So, when Proverbs 10:22 said, "The blessing of the LORD, it maketh rich, and he addeth no sorrow witn it," the author is simply saying that God will bless (heal and prosper) us without adding any impurities to those blessings, but He will address our impurities whenever His favor reveals them! Any sorrow that surfaces when God puts pressure on a certain dimension of us did not come from God; it came from sin. Think of it like this—if you had a puss-filled bump on your face and one of your parents decided to squeeze that bump, the parent simply put pressure on it. The pain you feel in that moment is the result of your skin conforming to your parent's touch. It is also the result of the infection underneath the skin. When pressure meets impurities, pain is inevitable! With enough pressure, the bump will pop, thus freeing that section of your skin, but this doesn't mean that your skin is now healthy and clean, after all, there is a reason that the bump surfaced in the first place. So, popping the bump cnly helped that section of your skin to start its healing process, but it did not deal with the underlying issue, nor dces it deal with the overall health of your skin. And, get this, you may not be ready to deal with the underlying issue just yet. Maybe, the problem is your diet. Then again, the issue could be the detergent you use to wash your bedding. All the same, the issue could be hormonal or it could be stress-related. And finally, you could be having an allergic reaction to something topical. There are many things that may have contributed to the infection of your skin, but it would take both time and testing to single out the issue or issues. And the issues could be layered, meaning you may end up changing your diet, and this may improve your skin's health, but you may notice that the bumps continue to surface from time to time. In short, you'd have to deal with the issue in layers. The same is true with God; the layers of our souls that we expose to Him, He will address and transform, but this is just the surface-level. Over time, God will go deeper and deeper in us until the entirety of who we are and what we've become is at the surface; this allows Him to separate the good from the evil within us. "For the word of God is living and active, sharper than any two-edged sword, piercing to the division of soul and of spirit, of joints and of marrow, and discerning the thoughts and intentions of the heart" (Hebrews 4:12/ESV).

Why did I use Tonya and Ashley's story as an example? For one, I want to dispel the belief that, as believers, we are "obligated" to share our formulas for success with other believers. We have to understand that it is God who promotes and prospers us. Our assignment to one another is to love one another, and one of the symptoms of love is support, but get this—we can't tell one another what support looks like to us. After all, there are believers out there who are angry with God because He did not support their ungodly relationships with narcissists and people who were sent by the enemy to destroy them. This is to say that if those people had it their way, they'd force God into supporting those relationships, and then they'd have the nerve to stand before Him whining and complaining about having been killed by their narcissistic lovers. Again, this is the "darned if you do; darned if you don't" predicament that we tend to place one another in. Ashley could have helped her friend, Tonya, by encouraging her to pray, and whenever Tonya heard back from God as to what He wanted her to do, Ashley could have supported her friend by cheering her on as she did it, and by giving her whatever aid she could have given her (within God's will). That's it and that's all! Tonya needed to find her authentic self, and the only way she would do this is if she sought out the heart of God, instead of chasing His hand. I immediately think about my dog and how he chases my hand whenever I have something in it that piques his interest, whether that thing is a treat or a toy. Once he gets what's in my hand, his interest in me diminishes as he turns his attention to what is now in his possession. Once he's consumed it or gotten bored with it, he turns his attention back to me, but not because he wants to learn my ways. He may look at me, hoping that I have more treats or more toys; then again, he may want attention. Either way, he's a sweet boy, but this does not diminish the fact that he's a canine.

One of my favorite scriptures to quote is Matthew 6:33, which reads, "But seek ye first the kingdom of God, and his righteousness; and all these things shall be added unto you." Having come out of dark pits of relational idolatry, I can truly say that God honors His promises to us! We all have a design; remember this statement. While we are made in the image of God, we all have a unique design in Him. Think about your natural face. No one on the face of this planet has your exact face, even if you're a twin. With twins, there are some differences that most of us don't necessarily see, but if you get to know a set of twins, triplets or quadruplets, over time, you'll be able to tell most of them apart, especially from up-close. You'll notice that one twin, for example, has a blood-spot on his left eye or the other twin's head (skull) may have a slight slope to it. One twin may have a scar from an accident, whereas another twin has a tendency to bite her lips or squint her eyes when she's intrigued. These quirks help us to differentiate one sibling from the other. I've found that in seeking God first, He gives us something that we all need to properly function in the Earth. We all have the ability to function, but most people do not and will never properly function in the Earth because they won't seek God first. To properly function on this planet, we need a revelation of who we are. When we think of the concept of purpose, we often think about what we're supposed to be doing when, in truth, purpose is not what we do, it's who we are. What we do is a product of what we believe. For example, I don't need healing, I am healed. Notice the words "I am."

- **Exodus 3:14 (ESV):** God said to Moses, "I am who I am." And he said, "Say this to the people of Israel, 'I am has sent me to you.'"
- **John 8:85 (ESV):** Jesus said to them, "Truly, truly, I say to you, before Abraham was, I am."

God refers to Himself as "I Am." Of course, we are created

in His image, therefore, anything we attach the prefix "I am" to, we shall have. For example, if you say, "I am blessed," you are coming into agreement with God as it relates to, not just how you are but who you are. If you say, "I am sick," you are coming out of agreement with Isaiah 55:3 (NJKV), which says, "But He was wounded for our transgressions, He was bruised for our iniquities; the chastisement for our peace was upon Him, and by His stripes we are healed." This is a part of our identity; we are healed. The more you know and embrace your identity, the less power Satan has over you. The more you acknowledge and declare who you are, the less power people's words will have over you. Going back to the Ashley/Tonya example, the moment Ashley saw that her friend was having an identity crisis, her job was to point Tonya back to Christ. For example, if I was Ashley, I probably would have said to Tonya, "Sis, you are beautifully and wonderfully made. There are so many layers of greatness in you, and God is simply peeling them back. When He does this, it can hurt, and sometimes, we think He's mad at us but, of course, this is not true. I'll support you on your entrepreneurial journey, but I don't want you to think that my path leads to success. My path will only lead me to success. Whatever path God has called you to will lead you to success, and hear me, success won't just be what you find; it's a revelation of who you are that you pick up along the way. You've just experienced a traumatic event; I understand this, but please don't take offense when I say this—don't let your trauma cause you to traumatize the people around you. You're putting me in a tight space. I want to help you, but I don't want to hinder you by helping you the way you want to be helped. You may be in survivor's mode right now; then again, you may be feeling vengeful, meaning you want to hurry up and access the realm of success so that you can rub your success in your former coworkers' faces. This is not the will of God for you, so let's try this—let me set up a therapy session for you with (insert therapist or counselor's name here). Also, let's be in prayer about where God wants to take you because I don't want you to try to lift the weights that God has given me. They may be too heavy for you right now. All the same, I think that God has something amazing in store for you and I don't want you to miss out on that." In this, Tonya will either become offended with me or she'll appreciate me all the more if she understands what I'm saying. If she grows angry with me, there's literally nothing I can do outside of giving her information that, quite frankly, won't benefit her in the end. In other words, I'd be wasting my time trying to help her fit into a space that God didn't carve out for her when I should have been helping her to find herself. Sure, I could give her practical business advice, for example, how to launch a website, how to locate her target audience and how to apply for an LLC, but it wouldn't be wise for me to tell her how to start a mousse line, especially when I've never heard her talk about doing so before. As a leader, I've seen this behavior many times and it almost always ends the same way. All the same, I've helped people in my life to discover the unique gifts that they have and how to tap into their potential. These people stick around and find success because it does not take them off their proper paths! Then again, I've literally had people to ask me how to do some or all of what I'm doing. When I was younger in the faith and bound by toxic loyalty, I would readily share the information, thinking I would be a bad friend by keeping it to myself. In one-hundred percent of those cases, those relationships ended because the people in question tried to walk a mile in my shoes and fell on their faces. I soon realized that I was not being a good friend to them by giving them what they wanted. I helped them to hurt and delay themselves, and for what?! Because I was afraid that if I didn't share the information with them, they'd classify me as a fake friend, and then they'd walk out of my life. In other words, I put my feelings over their mental health. Howbeit, when I grew out of this toxic way of reasoning, I became a true friend, and get this—every person in my intimate circle has found a measure of success! I learned that there is a thin line between helping people and hindering them, and if we are not careful, we'll partner with Satan by giving our friends and loved ones what they want, when they want it to their own destruction. This is called enabling.

Your God-given authority is linked to your authenticity; it is a product of you knowing and accepting who you are in Christ Jesus. God delivered me from the conformity found in today's traditional relationships and taught me how to be a genuine friend, confidante and associate to the people around me. I found my authority locked away in my authenticity, and the same is true for you. All the same, be mindful that you're not entertaining people who wrestle with comparison and competition. I'm not saying that you should disregard them altogether. I am saying that you shouldn't allow them into your intimate circle until they find God and ultimately find themselves.

YOUR INTIMATE CIRCLE VS. YOUR IMMEDIATE CIRCLE

Sometimes, we confuse our immediate circles with our intimate circle, and this type of confusion can be and oftentimes is costly! Jesus had 12 disciples; some of them were in His intimate circle but all of them were in His immediate circle. In short, they all had immediate access to Him, but not all of them could reach His heart. The reason this lesson is so important is because we are living in a time when most people don't understand how to have healthy relationships, and because of this, they try to access our intimate circles by rushing into our immediate circles. How many times have you allowed someone to have immediate access to you when that person did not have your heart? Think about that classmate-turned-friend who went out of her way to build a friendship with you, but the problem was that the building blocks she used were gossip. She talked about another student who didn't like you, and she used that student's hatred or disdain for you as a stepping stool to your heart. And while you saw great potential in her and you allowed her to walk, talk and sit with you everyday, you didn't trust her as far as you could see her. When people referred to her as your friend, you probably struggled with the term, trying to figure out the proper label to attach to your relationship with her, but over the course of time, you allowed the friendship label to stick. You started referring to her as your friend or maybe even your best friend, but one day, she gossiped about you and it got back to you. Your friendship with her gave up its pesky ghost, and you found it difficult to stop beating yourself up because the lesson wasn't necessary. You saw from the beginning that she didn't have the emotional capacity or maturity to be anyone's friend. And yet, you allowed her to rush into your immediate circle, and you allowed her and others to define your relationship with her, only for you to come back to the conclusion you'd made in the beginning. She wasn't a friend to anyone; she was fun to be around and she definitely had a lot of redeemable qualities, but her concept of loyalty was as loose as her lips.

Funny thing is, over the course of time, we have found ourselves meeting the conclusion of a matter before we tossed ourselves into the processes, only to come to that same conclusion years down the road. This is a part of life; it is the wilderness loop that we find ourselves in; that is until we come into agreement with God regarding whatever it is that He was attempting to tell us. In other words, we have to go in circles until our proverbial "ears to hear" finally open up. Until then, what we don't hear, we have to see and feel. Either way, the lesson will bring us to our knees in front of the Most High God.

- **Mark 4:23:** If any man have ears to hear, let him hear.
- **Revelation 3:22:** He that hath an ear, let him hear what the Spirit saith unto the churches.

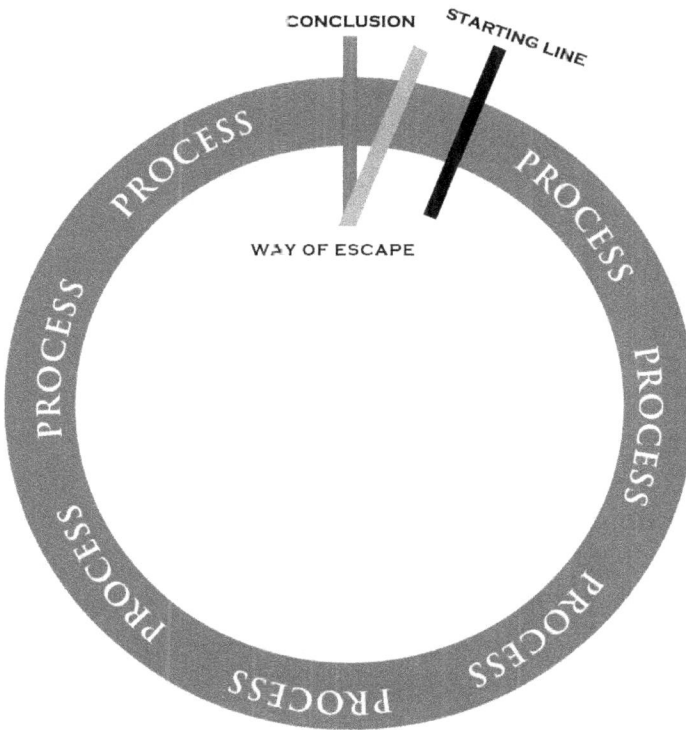

Notice in the above circle that we all start at a conclusion; that's the true starting line. But in order to see the conclusion, we have to know and believe what the Word of God says. If we are ignorant of His Word or we simply don't believe His Word, we will go past the conclusion and start a lengthy journey which will essentially lead us back to the same conclusion. Notice also that there is a way of escape; this is the window that the Most High gives us before we enter into a season of testing and warfare. Howbeit, if we don't take this window, we will start yet another journey around a mountain that God gave us the authority to move. Once we come around that mountain, we'll reach the same conclusion that we'd disregarded weeks, months, years or even decades ago! I've learned that this is why there are SO MANY people wrestling with unforgiveness out there. Yes, including professing Christians; this includes the seasoned ones! People have trouble forgiving other people when they have trouble forgiving themselves. "I knew that man was no good!" Charlotte shouts as she makes her way to the bathroom. "I saw all the signs, but nope! I had to go and date him anyhow! Now, look at me! Seven months pregnant by yet another deadbeat! When will I learn?!" And Charlotte may find herself angry with that ex for years, not because of the hurt and harm he brought to her life, but more so because he exposed a flaw in her system. He served as a painful reminder to Charlotte that she wasn't as confident as she pretended to be. She wasn't as discerning as she thought she was. The worst of them all was, her self-esteem wasn't as healthy as she thought it was. Now, Charlotte has to go through the motions all over again because she now needs to heal. The sad part is—Charlotte came to a conclusion about the guy she'd just parted ways with not long after she'd met him, but she didn't listen to the voice of discernement that echoed within her. All the same, this doesn't necessarily mean that she'll accept that truth regarding the next guy who makes his way into her life and ultimately into her heart. Realistically speaking, Charlotte will likely find herself in the same predicament three years later with a different guy, coming to the same conclusion. This process ends once she comes fully into agreement with God about her heart and her body.

Did you know that it is possible to marry someone and place that person in your immediate circle without giving him or her access to your intimate circle? This has been taking place for years. There are some women out there who are more open and honest with their friends than they are with their husbands. The same is true for the fellows. There are some men out there who are far more loyal to their friends than they are to their wives. This is the result of people confusing their intimate circles with their immediate circles. This is also to say that you should NEVER give intimate access to someone who only gives you immediate access to themselves. Consider the story of Martha and Mary. Luke 10:38-42 reads, "Now it came to pass, as they went, that he entered into a certain village: and a certain woman named Martha received him into her house. And she had a sister called Mary, which also sat at Jesus' feet, and heard his word. But Martha was cumbered about much serving, and came to him, and said, Lord, dost thou not care that my sister hath left me to serve alone? bid her therefore that she help me. And Jesus answered and said unto her, Martha, Martha, thou art careful and troubled about many things: But one thing is needful: and Mary hath chosen that good part, which shall not be taken away from her." In this, we can safely conclude that Martha gave Jesus immediate access to her heart, whereas Mary gave Him intimate access to hers. What's the difference? People who give you immediate access only make themselves accessible to you, but they aren't necessarily interested in your heart, your design, your plans or what you stand for. They are more interested in what you present or represent. People who have intimate access, on the other hand, are interested in you as a whole; they want to not only know what's in your heart, but they want to store it in their hearts as well. In short, they want to be one with you; they want to walk with you because they see the value of whatever it is that God has graced you to carry. For example, let's say that Shanice was a supervisor at her job, and two women had managed to penetrate her life and enter into her circle. One of those ladies is named Jamie and the other woman's name is Patricia, and both women are often seen walking alongside Shanice. The difference between the two women is this:

- Jamie is trying to learn everything that Shanice knows because she wants to ascend the ranks of the company and become a supervisor herself.
- Patricia wants to ascend the ranks, but she's not interested in learning anything new. Instead, she decided to link herself to the most powerful people in the office in hopes that they'll favor her enough to promote her.

One woman wants to learn; the other woman wants to manipulate her way into success. One woman wants to climb the ladder of success; the other wants to ride another person's coat tail. In this, we find that Jamie, professionally speaking, is a part of Shanice's intimate (professional) circle, but Patricia is a part of her immediate circle. If Shanice is not careful, she'll mess around and promote Patricia, and if this happens, Patricia will become her greatest enemy. This is because Patricia wasn't interested in what she had to offer as it relates to knowledge; she was only interested in what she stood to gain. Therefore, once Patricia accomplished what she'd set out to accomplish, Shanice would be of little to no importance to her. She may even consider Shanice a threat to her next level of promotion, so she may start trying to sabotage her former supervisor. This is why it is important to differentiate those who are a part of your intimate circle from the people who've managed to enter or slither into your immediate circle. A great example of this can be found in the book of Genesis. Abram allowed his nephew, Lot, to come with him on a journey that had only been carved out for him and the people in his care. While on this journey, Abram discovered why God said to him, "Get thee out of thy country, and <u>from thy kindred</u>, and from thy father's house, unto a land that I will shew thee" (see Genesis 12:1). Why would God tell you to walk away from your family? Abram discovered the answer to this question when Lot's herdsmen and Abram's herdsmen found themselves in a heated dispute. Genesis 13:2-7 reads, "And Abram was very rich in cattle, in silver, and in gold. And he went on his journeys from the south even to Bethel, unto the place where his tent had been at the beginning, between Bethel and Hai; Unto the place of the altar, which he had made there at the first: and there Abram called on the name of the LORD. And Lot also, which went with Abram, had flocks, and herds, and tents. And the land was not able to bear them, that they might dwell together: for their substance was great, so that they could not dwell together. And there was a strife between the herdmen of Abram's cattle and the herdmen of Lot's cattle: and the Canaanite and the Perizzite dwelled then in the land." Notice that the land was not able to bear both men and all of their riches. What happened here? By walking with Abram, Lot acquired a great deal of wealth and he soon proved that wealth without wisdom is truly a snare. And because Lot wasn't walking with God; instead, he was walking with Abram while Abram walked with God, Lot didn't have the wisdom or the revelation that God granted Abram access to. This is why he didn't understand that his wealth had been the product of his access to Abram. Because of this, he'd become so prideful that he'd allowed his herdsmen to challenge Abram's herdsmen, and he was silly enough to part ways with Abram, rather than correcting the men under his care. Consequently, Lot found himself in two predicaments, both of which Abram had to rescue him from:

- **The War in Sodom and Gomorrah** (Genesis 14:10–16): And the vale of Siddim was full of slimepits; and the kings of Sodom and Gomorrah fled, and fell there; and they that remained fled to the mountain. And they took all the goods of Sodom and Gomorrah, and all their victuals, and went their way. And they took Lot, Abram's brother's son, who dwelt in Sodom, and his goods, and departed. And there came one that had escaped, and told Abram the Hebrew; for he dwelt in the plain of Mamre the Amorite, brother of Eshcol, and brother of Aner: and these were confederate with Abram. And when Abram heard that his brother was taken captive, he armed his trained servants, born in his own house, three hundred and eighteen, and pursued them unto Dan. And he divided himself against them, he and his servants, by night, and smote them, and pursued them unto Hobah, which is on the left hand of Damascus. And he brought back all the goods, and also brought again his brother Lot, and his goods, and the women also, and the people.

- **Intercession for Sodom and Gomorrah** (Genesis 18:22–33): And the men turned their faces from thence, and went toward Sodom: but Abraham stood yet before the LORD. And Abraham drew near, and said, Wilt thou also destroy the righteous with the wicked? Peradventure there be fifty righteous within the city: wilt thou also destroy and not spare the place for the fifty righteous

    that are therein? That be far from thee to do after this manner, to slay the righteous with the wicked: and that the righteous should be as the wicked, that be far from thee: Shall not the Judge of all the earth do right? And the LORD said, If I find in Sodom fifty righteous within the city, then I will spare all the place for their sakes. And Abraham answered and said, Behold now, I have taken upon me to speak unto the Lord, which am but dust and ashes: Peradventure there shall lack five of the fifty righteous: wilt thou destroy all the city for lack of five? And he said, If I find there forty and five, I will not destroy it. And he spake unto him yet again, and said, Peradventure there shall be forty found there. And he said, I will not do it for forty's sake. And he said unto him, Oh let not the Lord be angry, and I will speak: Peradventure there shall thirty be found there. And he said, I will not do it, if I find thirty there. And he said, Behold now, I have taken upon me to speak unto the Lord: Peradventure there shall be twenty found there. And he said, I will not destroy it for twenty's sake. And he said, Oh let not the Lord be angry, and I will speak yet but this once: Peradventure ten shall be found there. And he said, I will not destroy it for ten's sake. And the LORD went his way, as soon as he had left communing with Abraham: and Abraham returned unto his place.

Note: Because Abram interceded on Lot's behalf, Lot and most of his family were saved from the destruction that came upon Sodom and Gomorrah. There's another lesson in this story, along with the story of Noah. Let's compare the two.

- **Genesis 19:30–38:** And Lot went up out of Zoar, and dwelt in the mountain, and his two daughters with him; for he feared to dwell in Zoar: and he dwelt in a cave, he and his two daughters. And the firstborn said unto the younger, Our father is old, and there is not a man in the earth to come in unto us after the manner of all the earth: Come, let us make our father drink wine, and we will lie with him, that we may preserve seed of our father. And they made their father drink wine that night: and the firstborn went in, and lay with her father; and he perceived not when she lay down, nor when she arose. And it came to pass on the morrow, that the firstborn said unto the younger, Behold, I lay yesternight with my father: let us make him drink wine this night also; and go thou in, and lie with him, that we may preserve seed of our father. And they made their father drink wine that night also: and the younger arose, and lay with him; and he perceived not when she lay down, nor when she arose. Thus were both the daughters of Lot with child by their father. And the firstborn bare a son, and called his name Moab: the same is the father of the Moabites unto this day. And the younger, she also bare a son, and called his name Benammi: the same is the father of the children of Ammon unto this day.

- **Genesis 9:20–25:** And Noah began to be an husbandman, and he planted a vineyard: And he drank of the wine, and was drunken; and he was uncovered within his tent. And Ham, the father of Canaan, saw the nakedness of his father, and told his two brethren without. And Shem and Japheth took a garment, and laid it upon both their shoulders, and went backward, and covered the nakedness of their father; and their faces were backward, and they saw not their father's nakedness. And Noah awoke from his wine, and knew what his younger son had done unto him. And he said, Cursed be Canaan; a servant of servants shall he be unto his brethren.

Moabites (ESV)	Ammonites	Canaanites
Numbers 25:1–5: While Israel lived in Shittim, the people began to	**Deuteronomy 23:3:** No Ammonite or Moabite shall	**Genesis 15:18–21:** On that day the LORD made a covenant with

177

Moabites (ESV)	Ammonites	Canaanites
whore with the daughters of Moab. These invited the people to the sacrifices of their gods, and the people ate and bowed down to their gods. So Israel yoked himself to Baal of Peor. And the anger of the LORD was kindled against Israel. And the LORD said to Moses, "Take all the chiefs of the people and hang them in the sun before the LORD, that the fierce anger of the LORD may turn away from Israel." And Moses said to the judges of Israel, "Each of you kill those of	enter the assembly of the Lord; none of their descendants, even to the tenth generation, shall ever enter the assembly of the Lord, **Judges 3:12–14:** And the children of Israel did evil again in the sight of the LORD: and the LORD strengthened Eglon the king of Moab against Israel, because they had done evil in the sight of the LORD. 13 And he gathered unto him the children of Ammon and Amalek, and went and smote Israel, and possessed the city of palm trees.	Abram and said, "To your descendants I give this land, from the Wadi of Egypt to the great river, the Euphrates—the land of the Kenites, Kenizzites, Kadmonites, Hittites, Perizzites, Rephaites, Amorites, Canaanites, Girgashites and Jebusites." **Genesis 24:3–4:** And I will make thee swear by the LORD, the God of heaven, and the God of the earth, that thou shalt not take a wife unto my son of the daughters of the Canaanites,

Moabites (ESV)	Ammonites	Canaanites
his men who have yoked themselves to Baal of Peor." **Judges 3:28**: And he said unto them, Follow after me: for the LORD hath delivered your enemies the Moabites into your hand. And they went down after him, and took the fords of Jordan toward Moab, and suffered not a man to pass over. **1 Kings 11:33**: Because that they have forsaken me, and have worshipped Ashtoreth the goddess of the Zidonians, Chemosh the god of the Moabites,	14 So the children of Israel served Eglon the king of Moab eighteen years. **Judges 11:4**: It came about after a while that the sons of Ammon fought against Israel. When the sons of Ammon fought against Israel, the elders of Gilead went to get Jephthah from the land of Tob; and they said to Jephthah, "Come and be our chief that we may fight against the sons of Ammon. **2 Samuel 10:7-10**: And when David heard of it, he sent Joab, and all the host of the	among whom I dwell: But thou shalt go unto my country, and to my kindred, and take a wife unto my son Isaac. **Numbers 14:43**: For the Amalekites and the Canaanites [are] there before you, and ye shall fall by the sword: because ye are turned away from the LORD, therefore the LORD will not be with you. **Numbers 21:3**: And the LORD hearkened to the voice of Israel, and delivered up

Moabites (ESV)	Ammonites	Canaanites
and Milcom the god of the children of Ammon, and have not walked in my ways, to do [that which is right in mine eyes, and [to keep] my statutes and my judgments, as [did] David his father.	mighty men. 8 And the children of Ammon came out, and put the battle in array at the entering in of the gate: and the Syrians of Zoba, and of Rehob, and Ishtob, and Maacah, were by themselves in the field. 9 When Joab saw that the front of the battle was against him before and behind, he chose of all the choice men of Israel, and put them in array against the Syrians: 10 And the rest of the people he delivered into the hand of Abishai his brother, that he might put them in array against	the Canaanites; and they utterly destroyed them and their cities: and he called the name of the place Hormah.

Joshua 3:10: And Joshua said, Hereby ye shall know that the living God [is] among you, and [that] he will without fail drive out from before you the Canaanites, and the Hittites, and the Hivites, and the Perizzites, and the Girgashites, and the Amorites, and the Jebusites. |

Moabites (ESV)	Ammonites	Canaanites
	the children of Ammon.	

Why did I share all of those scriptures? To show you that the greatest enemies of Israel were the ones who'd once been intimately or immediately connected to Israel. The Moabites and the Ammonites were descendants of Lot, Abraham's nephew. The Canaanites were descendants of Noah. In Matthew 10:34-36, Jesus said, "Think not that I am come to send peace on earth: I came not to send peace, but a sword. For I am come to set a man at variance against his father, and the daughter against her mother, and the daughter in law against her mother in law. And a man's foes shall be they of his own household." Of course, we all know what happened between Jesus and Judas Iscariot.

- **Matthew 26:20-21:** Now when the even was come, he sat down with the twelve. And as they did eat, he said, Verily I say unto you, that one of you shall betray me.
- **John 13:25-30:** He then lying on Jesus' breast saith unto him, Lord, who is it? Jesus answered, He it is, to whom I shall give a sop, when I have dipped it. And when he had dipped the sop, he gave it to Judas Iscariot, the son of Simon. And after the sop Satan entered into him. Then said Jesus unto him, That thou doest, do quickly. Now no man at the table knew for what intent he spake this unto him. For some of them thought, because Judas had the bag, that Jesus had said unto him, Buy those things that

we have need of against the feast; or, that he should give something to the poor. He then having received the sop went immediately out: and it was night.

- **Luke 22:47-48**: And while he yet spake, behold a multitude, and he that was called Judas, one of the twelve, went before them, and drew near unto Jesus to kiss him. But Jesus said unto him, Judas, betrayest thou the Son of man with a kiss?

The point that I'm making is, it is often the people who walked closest with you who will serve as your greatest enemies. Every leader has a Judas, an Absalom or a Delilah. These are the people who walk closely with us, but get this —most of them do not intentionally plan to betray us. What sets the stage for their ultimate betrayals is the conversations they've had with themselves and others. Remember, someone who enters your immediate circle is your Martha; that person is more concerned with who you are and what you can do for him or her. Martha-types will serve you until they feel you are of no benefit to them. They will honor you, speak highly of you and even buy you some of the most expensive gifts, but everything they do is self-motivated. These are the people that God spoke of in Proverbs 23:6-8, which reads, "Eat thou not the bread of him that hath an evil eye, neither desire thou his dainty meats: For as he thinketh in his heart, so is he: Eat and drink, saith he to thee; but his heart is not with thee. The morsel which thou hast eaten shalt thou vomit up, and lose thy sweet words. " Understand that you don't have their hearts because God doesn't have their hearts, therefore, it's not personal, it's spiritual. Ask any leader who has walked with God for an extensive amount of time, and those leaders will tell you that they've had their fair share of Delilahs, Absaloms and Judases. What's the difference between the three?

- **Delilah:** Delilahs know they are being used by the enemy. They have an objective and a goal, and all too often, they will pressure you to tell them things about you that could incriminate or humiliate you. They will incite conversations laced with gossip and slander in an attempt to get you to say something that they can ultimately use against you. They love keeping records of wrongs, therefore, they prefer to communicate through text messaging and emailing. Setting up a one-on-one, in-face discussion with them is not always easy, as they will claim to be too busy to meet up. They use seduction (tears, flattery, sex, etc.) to get what they want. They are accusers of the brethren who are always trying to ensnare believers. They will comfort you while you're down and even braid your hair, but their ultimate or overall objective is typically wealth related. Note: Delilahs are sent after you by the enemy.
- **Absalom:** Absaloms are typically loyal to you; that is until they deal with an offense that they can't seem to overcome. They will follow you, serve under your leadership faithfully (if you're a leader) and act as your greatest cheerleaders and supporters, but the minute they find fault in you, especially if you don't address the matter in a timely manner or in

the way they feel it should be addressed, they will distance themselves from you. After a few conversations with your enemies, they will convince themselves that you are not deserving of the platform on which you stand. They will then attempt to steal that platform from you by using your name to draw attention to themselves, and from there, they will seek to expose and destroy your character. These baby Jezebels are relentless and will not stop coming after you until they get entangled in a mess of their own. If you're not a leader or someone on a sizable platform, you likely don't qualify for an Absalom just yet, but if you plan to do anything great, beware. You will likely be used by the enemy to raise up your own Absalom. Note: Absaloms are raised and trained by you.

- **Judas:** These are the people who will walk with you just because of who you are, and like Absaloms, you likely won't qualify for a Judas until you've made some significant strides and accomplishments. The thing about Judas is—you can see them clearly! When they betray you, you are not surprised at all because they almost always seemed to be worried about carnal things. They are lovers of self and lovers of money; they are deceptive, cunning and prideful. They are absolutely unteachable! Nevertheless, they will walk with you for years, serving as your treasurer or within any capacity that you allow them to serve in. Unlike Absaloms, Judases don't want fame; they want fortune. They will typically betray you when an opportunity presents itself to them, and then play the victim once their deals with the devil don't produce the feelings or the results they hoped they'd yield.

Sadly enough, avoiding these three characters is not an easy task because, believe it or not, they are needed and necessary! Delilah was needed because she set the stage for Samson to bring down the Philistines. Absalom was necessary because his rebellion shed light on the fact that his father, David, hadn't been that great of a father. He'd stood by and said nothing after his son, Amnon, raped his daughter, Tamar. When the time came for him to choose the next king of Israel, he didn't sit by and allow his son, Adonijah to steal the throne. Instead, he elected and ordained Solomon as king in his stead. In other words, Absalom helped his father to stop being so passive with the people in his intimate circle. And, of course, Judas was needed because he set the stage for the death of Christ which, in turn, ushered in the New Testament. And without Christ's death, we couldn't have His resurrection, nor would we be resurrected in Him. This is to say that every enemy of yours serves a purpose. This doesn't mean that you should ignore the red flags that you see whenever people attempt to enter into your intimate, immediate or intellectual circles; it simply means that you need to forgive yourself for not seeing or properly responding to the ones who've already managed to enter your life and/or steal your heart. People in your intimate circle have access to your heart, whereas people in your immediate circle have access to your body, time and emotions. It goes without saying that anyone who has immediate access to you can manage to attain intimate access to you if that person says or does the right thing. This is why you have to be careful who you allow to walk closely with you. You should never intentionally train your Judas, nor should you ever entertain a Delilah knowing full-well that you're being manipulated and taken advantage of. And understand that there will be times when you'll suddenly realize that someone who has intimate or immediate access to you does not have your best interest at heart. What should you do when this happens? Move that person to your intellectual circle or out of your life altogether. How do you transition someone from your immediate or intimate circle to your intellectual circle?

1. Have a discussion with that person (if necessary). Explain why you are putting time, space and distance between yourself and that individual. Understand that the individual in question will gaslight you, love-bomb you or play the victim. Don't fall for this!

2. Take accountability for whatever it is that you've done wrong. Neglecting to do so could lead you into the realm of guilt, and guilt locks you into a reality that God has already delivered you from.

3. Introduce the person to the new norm. For example, I may say, "I love and appreciate you, and I don't want you to think that I'm diminishing anything you've done in my life, after all, I truly honor you! However, things have changed; I think we can both agree, and with that said, I won't be as available to you as I was in times past. Please hear me out—I am in no way putting you on punishment. I have no

desire to hurt you; my objective is to find a space for you in my life that you won't offend, and to find a space in your life that I can fit into comfortably. I'll be here whenever you need me, but I won't be opening my heart or home to you anymore. I sincerely hope that this doesn't offend you because I'm not discarding you. I'm just repositioning myself so that you can remain a part of my life, and vice versa."

Hard conversations are never easy, but hard situations are far worse. I've allowed people to barge into my immediate circle, and I've granted them measures of intimate access to my life, meaning I've told them things that I should not have told them. I've allowed these people to walk with me for months and even years before I came full circle to what God showed me the moment I'd laid eyes on them. Remember, we'll sometimes see the end result before we take the journey. This is to say that the journey wasn't necessary because the truth locked eyes with us and would not break its gaze, but we diverted our eyes and ignored the truth to follow after what we were told, what we felt and what we wanted. Consequently, we spent months and sometimes years returning to the conclusion that we once took for granted. One of the worst feelings to have usually surfaces when you discover that your finished line is your starting gate or springboard. It's when God shows you a truth that you refuse to see, so you run in circles until you're tired enough to see it.

Here's your challenge. Write down the names of the people closest to you. Understand that most of the people who are a part of your intimate circle are a part of your immediate circle, but a lot of the people in your immediate circle aren't a part of your intimate circle. On the paper or writing technology you've chosen to write the names on, test yourself and see if you can identify the who's who of your life. Who's a member of your intimate circle, and why? Who is a part of your immediate circle, and why? Now, ask yourself this—what circle do you believe that each of those people has placed you in? This is important because you may discover that you're hosting a series of one-sided relationships. Don't get me wrong. Some one-sided relationships are necessary, for example, it is not uncommon for us to give our pastors and therapists intimate access to us, but we don't know much about their personal lives, and that's simply the way it should be! So, I'm not saying that you should cut off everyone who has shut you out of what they consider to be sacred. I am, however, saying that you should be aware of where you stand with every person you entertain, just like you should be able to identify where those people stand with you. Keep in mind that ignorance means to ignore information that is readily present; it means to cover your eyes and be led by your feelings.

There's nothing wrong with having people in your immediate circle who are not a part of your intimate circle, but you need to be mindful of what you say to them and when you should avoid them altogether. For example, if you're living with your brother who happens to be ungodly, perverted and manipulative, that brother of yours would have immediate access to you, but this doesn't mean that you should give him intimate access. In other words, you shouldn't tell him what you're thinking, what your dreams are or any information that he could use against you. All the same, if you're sad, depressed, scared or angry, it would probably be a good idea if you avoided him altogether because when our souls are in states of distress, our hearts tend to open; this is how we form trauma bonds with other broken people. Consequently, you may tell your unsaved brother, for example, that your ex-boyfriend sent you a raunchy text message. This could incite him to pay that ex a visit and assault him, thereby landing him in jail. While you may feel your ex got what he deserved, what about your brother? Sometimes, we forget about the people who get caught in the crossfires of our poor decisions. Your objective should have been to demonstrate the love of God to your brother; your objective should never be to use his demons against someone else's demons. In other words, know what information to share with your brother versus what information to share with others. This is a part of having Godly relational acuity; it is the evidence of your maturity and your faith in God.

DEFEATING PASSIVITY

What is the definition of the word "passive"? According to Oxford Languages, the word "passive" can be defined as "accepting or allowing what happens or what others do, without active response or resistance." Again, we are multidimensional, multifaceted creatures, which means there are multiple sides to us. What you will discover is that there are some sides of you that are dominant, confident and in control; then again, there are some sides of you that are passive, insecure and out of control. What we have a tendency to do, as believers, is hide the sides of us that are not so secure, all the while, putting our best faces forward. When someone discovers our insecurities prematurely, we demote them in our lives or cast them out of our lives. This is especially true if we come in contact with a predatory person. Predatory people seek out the weaknesses and insecurities in others; they are masters at discovering the sides of people that they intentionally try to hide. Once they discover what they set out to discover, they then sink their fangs into their prey and begin to drain them, and while we could talk about how the world would be a better place without predatory people, the better argument would be how the world would be better off if we, simply put, gave no place to the devil. In other words, predatory people would not exist if they didn't have something or someone to prey on, therefore, the objective is not to rid the world of them. The objective is for us to wake up, sober up and stand up against the wiles of the devil. The objective is for us to realize who we are in Christ, but first, we have to realize who He is, not just in title, but in heart. In other words, we have to build intimate relationships with the Lord. A lot of believers have invited Jesus into their intellectual circles and their immediate circles, but they have not invited Him into their hearts. Isaiah 29:13 (ESV) reads, "And the Lord said: "Because this people draw near with their mouth and honor me with their lips, while their hearts are far from me, and their fear of me is a commandment taught by men."

I was just getting a little traction in my journey as an entrepreneur. A year prior to this, I'd launched my first business venture, and in 2008, I'd finally found my footing. At that time, I was SUPER PASSIVE when it came to authority figures. I mean, I had it BAD! I suspect that this is because I'd never seen a great example of leadership outside of my pastor at that time, plus, my parents put a lot of emphasis on honoring our elders and those in authority. And while I am super grateful that they taught us about honor and respect, I can truly say that they caused us to have the wrong perspective of authority figures because of what we witnessed with them. This translated into me being super passive with people in authority, but for my siblings, it caused them to hate authority figures, therefore, they rebelled against authority. I'd had my taste of what it was like to be an entrepreneur, and after having an incredibly horrific experience with a client of mine, I was at a crossroads in entrepreneurship. On one hand, I wanted to continue growing my business and growing as an entrepreneur but, on the other hand, I was beginning to think that the business world just wasn't for me. The crazy thing was—I didn't fear authority, I feared myself. I was afraid of what could potentially come out of me, and what that would do to my future. In other words, I was afraid I'd say or do the wrong thing. However, after working with an incredibly narcissistic and controlling client, I knew that I couldn't go back to wearing a muzzle if I wanted to remain in business. I ended up meeting a girl (we'll call her Trina), and Trina had reached out to me wanting to have a logo designed. We spoke over the phone about what she wanted, and when I believed I'd grasped it, I disconnected the line and went straight to work. Of course, Trina paid me a deposit before I'd gotten started. After the logo was completed, I sent it to Trina and she loved it! She called me to express just how much she loved her new logo, and somehow, the conversation moved from the professional realm to the personal one (I've since learned better, of course). Trina told me about her life, her business ventures and her plans. She shared story after story with me about her time as an entrepreneur, and even though she'd closed her former business, she was ready to start a new one. I told her about some of my business dealings, and she kept responding with, "It couldn't have been me!" She told me how she would have responded to those clients and I laughed at her boldness. She hired me again, and from there, a friendship began to blossom.

One day, I got a wild idea. What if I brought Trina in as a partner in my business? Sure, she didn't know how to design websites, but she knew the language of the business world, plus she didn't mind going toe-to-toe with people. I didn't want to fight with anyone; I just wanted to create websites and logos, and I wanted to have fun doing so. In other words, I didn't want to develop my teeth in the business world. I wanted everything to remain soft. I wanted the fruit of entrepreneurship, but I didn't want to develop the roots needed to anchor me in that world. All the same, I was convinced that the idea had come from God, so I called Trina and told her about my idea. "I'm getting chills," she said. She went on to explain to me that she'd had a similar idea. With those words, we both concluded that God wanted us to become business partners, so we started talking about the legal portion of it all. Before long, we'd picked a name for our new business, applied for an EIN number, set the date for the grand opening and spent hours upon hours on the phone talking about our new venture. I logged into my web design host, purchased a new URL and attached it to the new and improved site I'd just created for Trina and I. The plan was for Trina to get Photoshop and start learning how to use it. She was also supposed to practice building websites using the web builder site I'd sent her. Trina and I had just become business partners, and we were well on our way to becoming best friends.

A week or two before the grand opening, I got hired by a guy who wanted me to design his website and, of course, I happily obliged. The problem was, however, he wanted a flash site. I didn't know anything about flash. Of course, flash sites are now a thing of the past, but they were considered the top shelf sites of that era. "No worries," the client told me. "You can use Wix to build my site." I'd heard of Wix, but I wasn't familiar with its builder, so I was a little hesitant, nevertheless, I needed the money, plus, I wanted to learn as much as I could, so I agreed to design his site. The site came out amazing! I was taken aback with how professional, clean and beautiful his site was, and even more honored that I'd had the privilege of designing it. Once his order was complete, I had about a week or less before the grand opening of my new business venture with Trina, so I decided to surprise her. I went to Wix, signed up for an account and began to design our new site over there. "She's going to love this," I thought to myself as I watched the site come together. My plan was to transfer the domain to the new site the day before the grand opening and then call Trina to tell her the great news. I imagined how excited she'd be seeing the new and improved site. Every night, I stayed up late (which is a norm for me) to build the new site, and I must say, I was loving it! And finally, the day of reveal came. I'd transferred the domain to our new site and I called Trina when I got off work that day. She didn't answer her phone, but no worries. I knew she'd call me back when she was available. I started driving to Gloria's house to hang out with her; Gloria was my best friend at that time. I remember pulling up in the parking lot of Gloria's apartment when my phone started ringing. I'd left Trina a voicemail telling her to check out our new site, so when I saw her name on my caller I.D, I remember smiling. I was sure I'd hear the sound of her screaming for joy when I answered the phone, but I was wrong. Trina sounded dry. I mean, she sounded extra offended, but she wasn't raising her voice. This was our first day as business partners, so I expected her to be a little more jovial, but she seemed to be in a not-so-pleasant mood. I have to also mention that she lived states away from me. "Did you hear my voicemail?" I asked excitedly. "Yeah, I heard it," Trina said in the driest, most unappealing tone. I was confused. I was sitting in my car waiting to finish my conversation with Trina so I could go and knock on Gloria's door, but I realized that I wasn't going to be getting out of that car as soon as I'd planned. "What's wrong?" I asked as I pulled my leg back into my vehicle and closed the door. "Don't you like the new site?" Trina cleared her throat before letting me know how she felt. That day was the first day I'd ever experienced her yelling at me. "It looks good, but ... wait. Nevermind." The smile on my face immediately turned upside-down. "What's wrong?" I asked. "Tell me." Trina sighed before responding. "You didn't think to inquire of me before you made changes to OUR site?!" she asked. "We are business partners now! Anything you do to that site, you must have my permission! This is like a marriage! You can't go and make changes without consulting with me first!" I sat in the car frustrated, confused, but more than anything, realizing that I'd just made a huge mistake. "Trina, you don't know how to design websites," I countered. "We talked about this. The plan is for you to learn while I continued building. Besides, I work by inspiration, and that inspiration typically comes in the middle of the night, so are you telling me that now, if I feel inspired, I have to wait for you to wake up to get your permission before I do anything with our site?!" I was definitely ready to serve Trina with a writing of entrepreneurial divorcement in that moment. All the same, I genuinely wanted her to see my side of the coin before responding. "Yes, that's exactly what I'm saying!" she shouted. "You are no longer in business by yourself! You and I are married in business! Anything you do to OUR business, you must first consult with me!" We went back and forth for about thirty minutes to an hour, but I would not back down because I understood that doing things the way Trina wanted me to do them would be entrepreneurial suicide for me. I serve on the third shift. The anointing comes over me at night when everyone is at rest; this is when I get my greatest ideas and strategies. This is when my energy is at its peak, and during this time, Trina was always sound asleep. A lot of designers have this issue. When Trina realized that I wasn't going to agree to her new world order, she said to me, "Well, it's your business. Once I realize that I'm not getting anywhere with people, I give up." It was the first day of us being in business together, and just like that, I was back in business by myself, but her name was now on my business as well. We had an EIN number. I didn't press for her to reconsider because I realized that Trina felt the need to be in charge of everything, and I can truly say I don't do well with controlling people. All the same, she was partially right. I had to confess this to myself. I was no longer in business for myself, but how could she not contribute a dime to the business and then think that I was supposed to ask for her permission just to do what I'd been doing for years? I can't submit to control; I submit to Godly authority. Trina and I didn't talk about the issue anymore for more than a year. Instead, she started practicing with Photoshop and playing with the design software while I continued to build and grow the business. About a month or two later, Trina stopped promoting the business altogether, and she'd moved on to other business ventures. Of course, I regretted my decision to shut down my first business to re-brand and relaunch it, but I can truly say now that I needed that lesson. What was the lesson here? I was running from dying to myself. I wanted the perks of the business world, but not the hard stuff that came with being an entrepreneur, so I brought someone into my business that had no experience and hadn't made a single contribution towards the business, and I gave her equal rank with myself. When she'd gotten that rank, she started trying to boss me around. And again, she was right, albeit, partially. In a partnership, you have to consider your partner when making decisions. In another way, she was wrong because we'd discuss (to no ends) how I worked before that great and awful day, and she hadn't said a thing! I continued to build the business for over a year before I decided to legally part ways with Trina. I was living in Germany by then, so I'd elected to call her when I knew she was awake. I told her about my concerns. I remember saying to her, "You haven't touched or talked about this business in more than a year." She agreed. She echoed the words she'd said on our opening day a year prior. "Once I realize that I'm not getting anywhere with people, I quit." Thankfully, she didn't mind us dissolving the business. I decided to close it altogether and launch my own web design company under a new name and a new EIN number, and I built a whole new site for my company. Over the course of time, I had to allow God to develop my teeth in the business world. Looking back, it's funny to me how "flowery" I was, meaning how soft and naive I was. I can genuinely say that I am nowhere near that same girl today. I grew up. I got stronger. I established boundaries, and now I teach others how to do the same. You see, we often think that our issues are a part of our personalities when they are not. Our issues arrest, limit and deform our personalities, but they are not who we are. I was nowhere near passive with Trina because passivity was not who I was, it's how I became. And the more I did business with cantankerous, manipulative and rebellious people, the more my true personality surfaced. My first years in full-time business were hilarious. When I think back to all the mistakes I made, the encounters I had and the rules I implemented to keep those problems from resurfacing, I get a good laugh from it all. This is why whenever I come across new business owners who are super passive and afraid of the business world, I always tell them, "No worries. You won't stay that way if you continue on in business." What was I saying? Simply put, productivity strengthens your spine and it helps you to overcome passivity.

What is the soul comprised of again? The mind, will and emotions, right? To be passive simply means that your will is weak. Your will, of course, is the third dimension of your soul. How does a person's will become weak? The answer is simple—your will becomes weak whenever you don't repeatedly exercise it. It becomes weak when you repeatedly allow others to eclipse your will with their own. It becomes weak when you don't speak up for yourself. It becomes weak when you allow others to control and manipulate you. Howbeit, being weak-willed is not a personality trait. It's a deficiency of faith. It is usually centered around you being afraid of what others may say or think about you, and believe it or not, if you are weak-willed, you have people in your life who are only there because they have a measure of control over you in one area or another. Keep in mind that control is not always overt or over the top; sometimes, it's covert or, better yet, undercover or underneath the surface. Overt controllers will raise their voices or use their heightened emotions to get what they want; they will typically try to intimidate you into doing whatever it is that they want you to do. Covert controllers use the illusion of kindness, passivity and fear to get their way. They try to pass you off as the controlling one; this is why covert controllers typically try to get around people who are louder and more confident than themselves. This allows them to pass themselves off as weaker and more vulnerable. This usually works with onlookers because most people run to the defense of anyone they feel is being bullied. A covert controller will use tears, gaslighting and the illusion of victimhood to manipulate the people around them.

Productivity or being super productive as it relates to your gift and your responsibilities is a powerful weapon against passivity because it helps you to grow your passion, and get this, passion eclipses passivity. It also helps you to develop the language for any given world that you enter. You see, when I was passive with authority figures, it was because I was raised under a culture that dictated that I wear a muzzle in the presence of people in authority, and while I am a huge proponent for order and honor, I believe that my parents didn't give us any balance in that area. Consequently, we had no language or understanding of honor; we simply learned to move in it without asking any questions, but honor without understanding produces passivity. Think about it. It is the very thread that makes up religion without relationship. It sets the stage for passive believers to surface, fearing the wrath of God while having no true understanding regarding the heart or nature of God. In short, people accept what they hear without studying for themselves or, at least studying the entirety of the Bible. Having studied with a few Christian denominations, I came to the conclusion that most denominations and religious sects choose sections of the Bible to highlight and read from, all the while ignoring the rest of God's Word. They put emphasis on the scriptures that seem to validate their core beliefs, but they stay away from anything that challenges what they've come to believe. This is why it is important for us to read the Bible for ourselves and to seek God outside of the traditional church. Yes, you should go to church; don't mistake what I'm saying, but your relationship with God should not be established through a third-party (your pastor or religion). Some people's Bibles live in the backseats of their vehicles, and are only touched on Sunday morning when they are being dragged out at church. I've also noticed that a LOT of the people who've complained to me about enduring repeated excessive warfare, when questioned, have admitted to me that they don't read their Bibles as often as they should. Nevertheless, they seek out therapists and mentors, hoping to supplement their Bible study with long talks about what they're going through, not realizing that the answers to their problems can be found in their very neglected Bibles. In other words, they go the long way to a conclusion.

THE RETURN OF THE UNCLEAN SPIRIT

"When the unclean spirit is gone out of a man, he walketh through dry places, seeking rest, and findeth none. Then he saith, I will return into my house from whence I came out; and when he is come, he findeth it empty, swept, and garnished. Then goeth he, and taketh with himself seven other spirits more wicked than himself, and they enter in and dwell there: and the last state of that man is worse than the first. Even so shall it be also unto this wicked generation" (Matthew 12:43-45). What do you imagine happening when you read this passage of scripture? If you're like most believers, you imagine a demon being cast out of a person, wandering around in the Earth, and then deciding to go back to the person it was evicted from. You imagine it finding the person, and the individual has not done the work to justify or sustain his or her deliverance. You then imagine that same devil going out and about, partnering with seven more spirits before returning to the person it was cast out of. The individual would end up getting bound once again, but this time, the individual would be in worst condition than he or she was in initially. If this is what you imagine when reading this scripture, you're not entirely wrong. Nevertheless, there is more to this particular passage than meets the eye. For example, the unclean spirit isn't walking down the street looking for a new host. The Bible says the evil spirit walks through dry places. The word "dry" is defined as "free from moisture

or liquid; not wet or moist" (Oxford Languages).
Understand this—the Greek word for "spirit" is "pneuma,"
and it means "wind, breath, spirit" (Source: Strong's
Concordance). When God formed Adam's body, the Bible
tells us that He breathed the breath of life into man, and
man became a living soul. We are spirits living in bodies.
What about an unclean spirit? It's a fallen angel or, better
yet, a demon. Going back to the aforementioned scripture,
the dry places referenced in Matthew 12:43 are lifeless
places or, better yet, inanimate objects. As I mentioned in
Relational Acuity 4.0, demons are like cell phones. The
Bible refers to God as Light (see 1 John 1:5); He is also
Abba, which means "Source." Therefore, God is the Source
of all power; this is why He is All-Powerful. Again, demons
are like cellphones. When they rebelled against God, they
found themselves disconnected from the Source of all
power, and like cell phones, they began to power down.
They had some light left, but being cast into darkness (out
of God's presence), they found that what was left of this
light was quickly diminishing. They needed something to
inhabit that was like them (spirits), so when they saw
mankind in the Earth, they got a not-so-bright idea. Satan
borrowed the body of a snake and then made his way into
the Garden of Eden. There, he deceived Adam and Eve, and
just like that, the couple fell dimensionally, giving Satan
and his imps legal access to them. This allowed demons to
usurp the authority of humans and, of course, Jesus came
and restored this authority to us. Howbeit, we still have to
use it.

Resurfacers. That's the label I created for the people who

go out of my life, and then at some point, try to resurface. This typically happens when I'm transitioning from one season to the next or if I'm working on some major project that God has given me. I've learned to study the patterns of the enemy, not just in general, but in my personal life. This helps me to identify areas in my life that need to be fortified with boundaries and covered in prayer. Resurfacers are annoying. They typically walk away when they feel they no longer need you, and they always try to resurface when they are in the midst of a storm, when they want something from you or when they see that you have accomplished some great feat. They also resurface when they want to be nosy. What's worse is they don't bother hiding their intentions. They will say, for example, "Girl, I thought about you today and I said to myself, let me go look her up on Instagram! Imagine how shocked I was when I saw pictures of your new car, your new man and your new house! I am so proud of you!" From there, they will try to catch up on things with you, hoping that you will allow them to reenter your life if, but for a moment. But what if I told you that this is one of the ways that unclean spirits return? Any time I've conducted a deliverance session, especially a mass deliverance session, I have warned the people to keep all shut doors shut! By this, I mean—don't allow Satan to throw people at you. Sometimes, the easiest way for a familiar spirit to reenter your life is by using a person that you're familiar with. How does this work? Imagine that you have a car, and so does your coworker. Your coworker's car is repossessed and she doesn't have the money to reclaim it, so she asks you to take her to work. Your car is the vehicle that gets her from her house to the office, and from the office to her house, but it's still your car. Not having a car did not stop her from going to work; she just had to find another way to get there. In this, the resurfacer is the vehicle by which the enemy seeks to reenter your life.

Resurfacers don't always pop up after a successful deliverance session; they typically arise when you're in the midst of a change, for example, you may be shifting from one season to the other. Keep in mind that a season is comprised of both time and beliefs; it is a time in which you are locked into a certain vault of revelation and information. When God opens that vault, He gives you access to new information for a period of time. This, again, is a season. Nevertheless, that vault is inside of another vault, meaning once you've gotten what you need from that season, God will grant you access to more information and wisdom. When you're about to leave an old way of thinking behind, resurfacers tend to show up in the forms of ex-lovers, former friends and estranged family members. If you haven't shifted a lot in life, you've probably never experienced this, but any person who has grown in Christ repeatedly can testify about folks who suddenly reappeared after having been gone from their lives for years on end. I've taught this truth in some of my writers' classes, and what amazes me the most is that I've had students to fall into these traps after having been warned. I've gotten inbox messages that read like, "Ms. Tiffany! You were right! I received a text message from my ex, and get this, I haven't heard from that man in five years!" This is fine, but what shocks me is that the woman in question will still entertain the guy! Anytime I've witnessed this happen, the woman (or man) will not finish his or her book because the writer is suddenly being distracted and entertained by the ex or the resurfacer. Does the resurfacer stick around? Nope. I've seen cases where they've stuck around for years, only to leave after they've further damaged the people. This is why I highly advise people to heal, forgive and move forward; this way, Satan can't find them where he left them. Let me explain it this way. Your exes, your former friends and every person who has ever exited your life could relate to you in one dimension or another. Let's not forget that, as humans, we are multifaceted, multidimensional beings. With that being said, in one or more of those areas, you agreed with the ex or the fallen friend. What you agreed about may have been a lie or a series of lies; then again, your agreement may have been based on your immaturity and brokenness at one point in your life. Maybe your ex told you that, like you, he wanted to travel the world, feed the homeless, have a stable and Godly marriage and move to Texas, meaning he was mirroring what you told him. What is mirroring? Psychology Dictionary reported the following about mirroring:

> "Mirroring is the process of emulating, or copying exactly the behaviors, speech, and characteristics of another individual. Therapists can sometimes employ mirroring techniques to come across as empathizing with their patients."

Narcissists mirror their victims and their intended victims. The following information was taken from the Narcissist

Family Files:

> "People with narcissistic personality disorder (NPD), on the other hand, take mirroring to extremes. Because they lack a stable and sustaining sense of identity and self-worth, narcissists forever look to external sources for definition and esteem. When they find a prospective or new partner, they study that person and attempt to reflect back their personality, style, interests, and values. If you like going to the gym, gardening, chocolatey desserts, and helping at the local animal shelter, so do they! If you have tattoos, suddenly they show up with one too" (Source: Narcissist Family Files/Life in the Fun House: Narcissistic Mirroring and Projection/Julie L. Hall).

Again, what you agreed with the ex or former friend about could have been a lie; maybe they mirrored your behavior, presenting themselves as the answer to your prayers. Then again, they may have emerged like super heroes to rescue you in your hour of distress. Either way, they came into your life, hurt and disappointed you, and then promptly exited your life. And now, all of a sudden, you have received a text from the ex, and you're wondering what spiked his or her sudden change of heart. The answer isn't important. What is important is that the ex doesn't find you in the same mindset that he or she left you in. In other words, what once connected you to your ex should no longer be what reconnects you. If you were a drinker and you bonded with your ex because he or she loved to drink, that ex should find you completely sober. If you were a gossiper and your former friend bonded with you over the latest news about someone's life, should she try to reemerge, she shouldn't still find you gossiping. You could easily repel her by simply responding to her gossip about another person by saying, for example, "Oh wow. That's horrible news. Bow your head; let's pray for her right quick." James 4:7 reads, "Submit yourselves therefore to God. Resist the devil, and he will flee from you." In this, your former gossiping friend will rush off the phone and out of your life because she'll feel humiliated, offended and confused.

The point is:
1. Once God shuts a door, don't reopen it.
2. Once God shuts a door, don't open a window.
3. Once God shuts a door, don't drill a hole in it.
4. Once God shuts a door, don't unlock it.
5. Once God shuts a door, don't crack it open.

The unclean spirits that would seek to return to your life need doors (legal access) or windows (illegal access). Don't give them either! This brings to mind a dream I had earlier this year (or late last year; I'm not sure). In the dream, I was playfully riding on someone's back (I think it was my older brother). My sister was walking alongside us and we were all laughing and having a great time. We were walking into the apartment we'd lived in when we were younger (I was between the ages of 12 and 21). It was dark outside. As my brother carried me into the house, I noticed a bush outside that was moving. I could tell that someone was using the bush to disguise themselves, and I assumed that it was someone we were familiar and friendly with, and that person was playing a practical joke on us, so I wasn't alarmed when the bush followed us into the apartment. I wanted to see who was in it, so as my brother carried me down the hallway, I kept looking back at the bush that was now following us. At some point, I realized that I didn't know whoever was in the bush, so I got off my brother's back, and when I did this, the bush began to shrink. I then picked the bush up, took it to the living room door and tossed it outside. That's when some tall guy came out of the bush. I don't remember what he looked like; I just remember that he was unpleasant. I closed the door and locked it; that's when he started shooting through the door. I remember watching parts of the door explode as the bullets flew in, but none of those bullets touched me or either of my siblings. What did this dream represent? My siblings were in the dream, so it dealt with a generational issue. That guy in the bush represented a familiar spirit. It had obviously been cast out of my family because it had to disguise itself to get into my mother's apartment. Note: my mother wasn't home in the dream. Once I got off my brother's back, it began to shrink. Riding my brother's back was likely symbolic of me allowing someone else to carry me around in the spirit, but once I stood on my own two feet, that demon began to shrink; this is because my faith had grown. I then picked the bush-covered-devil up like it was a tiny but nasty rag, and I threw it out the door before closing the door. This represents deliverance. What God was showing me was that He'd used me to cast out a generational issue that had been plaguing my bloodline for generations on end, and that devil was mad! He'd formed his weapons, but they did not prosper. In short, the dream warned me of an unclean spirit that had attempted to return, but its plans had been thwarted once I recognized my own authority.

What about you? Answer the following questions (if they pertain to you):

1. How often do you allow exes to return to your life?
2. What about your former friends?
3. What events or occasions preceded someone from your past reentering or attempting to reenter your life?
4. What events or occasions succeeded or followed the return of these people?
5. How long did the resurfacers in your life stuck around, and are you still entertaining them?
6. In what areas or dimensions are you connected with these people? (Example: gossip, loneliness, common enemy, etc.).
7. What benefit do you get from entertaining the resurfacers in your life?
8. What would it take for you to close those doors once and for all?

Understand this—when a person resurfaces in your life, that person has unfinished business with you, whether good or bad. Don't reopen closed doors unless God says otherwise, after all, you may be welcoming a spirit that failed in its assignment against you the first time, and you may be giving it another shot at you. Love wisely.

DARK PSYCHOLOGY

What is dark psychology? "Dark Psychology is the art and science of manipulation and mind control. While Psychology is the study of human behavior and is central to our thoughts, actions, and interactions, the term Dark Psychology is the phenomenon by which people use tactics of motivation, persuasion, manipulation, and coercion to get what they want" (Source: Dr.JasonJones.com/Dark Psychology & Manipulation: Are You Unknowingly Using Them?). In short, dark psychology is the study of the human desire to control other humans. One of the mistakes many of us make, as believers, is we don't study psychology. Most believers don't even study their Bibles. Because of this, we tend to have encounters with dark personality types; yes, even in the church, and we don't always know how to navigate those encounters. Consequently, a lot of former church-goers have chosen to forsake the coming together of the saints in favor of watching their local assemblies' services online. The truth of the matter is—a lot of believers don't care to learn about the many tactics, wiles, tools and techniques of the devil. In other words, we choose to remain ignorant, hoping that this ignorance will somehow make us untouchable, especially if we pair it with a bunch of declarations that we've learned from our favorite celebrity pastors. This has resulted in a lot of Christians turning away from the faith, thinking that it's all a sham when, in truth, they tried to treat the Word of God like words. What does this mean?

They thought they could use scriptures and well-formed words to stop Satan from acting like Satan, and when their religious spells didn't work, they got angry, denounced the faith and went back into the world. Some of them even started practicing witchcraft, hoping that it would give them quicker and more effective results, and they did this to provoke God because of their anger towards Him.

Understanding what lurks in the darkness will undoubtedly help you to test the spirits that attempt to enter or reenter your life. Think of it this way. Let's pretend that you are a skilled chess player. You've become so skilled at the game of chess that you don't care to play it anymore because you beat most people at the game in a matter of minutes (that's if they don't delay all of their plays). Howbeit, one of your friends convinces you to play the game with his father, claiming that his dad is one of the best chess players around. You've heard claims like these before, and at first, you'd rejected his offer, but after he kept bragging about his father's skills, you finally decided to play, at minimum, a single round of chess with the guy. The day comes and your friend brings his father to your house as planned. Mr. Nelson (your friend's father) walks into your living room and sits in front of your chess table. "Let's get this over with," he says. "It's two o'clock. I should be done spanking you by 2:30. Hope you wore a diaper." Mr. Nelson is definitely confident in his abilities; it becomes more and more evident to you that the elderly gentleman has not seen many losses. Excited to finally have what you deem as some "real competition," you sit your soda down and make your way to the other side of the chess table. "I usual y respect the elderly," you joke. "But today, I'm going tc turn your dentures upside down." Mr. Nelson smiles. Like you, he's tired of playing with rookies. "I like you," he says before pulling a huge cigar out of his jacket. "I almost wish I had claimed you when you were growing up." The two of you laugh as you arrange the chess pieces. An hour and twenty minutes later, you stand to your feet to mock your opponent with a playful yawn. "Sorry, Mr. Nelson," you laugh. "I've checkmated you twenty minutes ago and you're still sitting there. I don't know if I need to help you up or if rigor mortis has already set in." Your friend laughs. "Leave my Dad alone," he says. "He's still in shock." What happened here? Simply put, if this story were true, it would mean that you are an incredibly skilled chess player. It would also mean that you know the ins, the outs and the tricks found in chess. You've learned how to strategically move your pieces on the board, you've learned how to read the body language of your opponent and you've learned how to fake your own body language to sway your opponent. How did you become so good at the game? You kept playing and studying it, right?! Unlike most people, you didn't stop playing the game during the stage or phase when you kept losing (the learning curve). You kept playing, studying and learning as much as you could about the game, and even when you became good at it, you didn't allow yourself to become satisfied because you wanted to be the best chess player around. Eventually, you became so good at the game that you didn't care to play it anymore because it was difficult for you to meet an opponent that even remotely matched your level of skill. This is how God wants us to be as it relates to the kingdom of darkness. Satan attacks us; we understand this, but did you know that Satan has no new tricks? This means that if you learn his patterns, his weaknesses and his favorite strategies, you'll be able to predict and counter many of his movements. Over time, your faith will grow so much that you may find yourself responding in the same manner that Jesus responded after hearing of Lazarus' sickness. John 11:1-6 reads, "Now a certain man was ill, Lazarus of Bethany, the village of Mary and her sister Martha. It was Mary who anointed the Lord with ointment and wiped his feet with her hair, whose brother Lazarus was ill. So the sisters sent to him, saying, 'Lord, he whom you love is ill.' But when Jesus heard it he said, 'This illness does not lead to death. It is for the glory of God, so that the Son of God may be glorified through it.' Now Jesus loved Martha and her sister and Lazarus. So, when he heard that Lazarus was ill, he stayed two days longer in the place where he was." Of course, we know the rest of this story. Lazarus died, and by the time Jesus went to his tomb, he'd been dead for four days. Nevertheless, Jesus proved that there is nothing too hard for Him by raising Lazarus from the dead. This is a powerful demonstration of faith! Not only did He allow Lazarus to pass away, Jesus didn't go to see him until his body had already started the decomposition process! While this was not a demonstration of dark psychology, Jesus demonstrated to us that we have power over death.

One component of dark psychology is called the dark triad. The following information was taken from Psychology Today:

"The term "Dark Triad" refers to a trio of negative personality traits—narcissism, Machiavellianism, and psychopathy—which share some common malevolent features. The construct was coined by researchers Delroy L. Paulhus and Kevin M. Williams in 2002" (Source: Psychology Today/Dark Triad).

The Dark Triad		
Narcissism	Machiavellianism	Psychopathy
Narcissism, patholo gical self-absorption, first identified as a mental disorder by the British essayist and physician Havelock Ellis in 1898. Narcissism is characterized by an inflated self-image and addiction to fantasy, by an unusual coolness and composure shaken only when the narcissistic confidence is threatened, and by the tendency to take others for granted or to exploit them. The	Machiavellianism is not a mental health diagnosis; rather, it's a personality trait describing a manipulative individual who deceives and tricks others to achieve goals. It is based on the political philosophy of the 16th-century writer Niccolò Machiavelli. Some evidence suggests that of the dark traits, Machiavellian ism is most closely tied to high intelligence. If a psychologist refers to someone as 'High Mach,' it means	Psychopathy is a personality disorder defined by a constellation of affective and behavioral symptoms. The symptoms of psychopathy include shallow affect; lack of empathy, guilt and remorse; irresponsibility; impulsivity; and poor planning and decision-making (Kiehl & Hoffman, 2011). The best current estimate suggests that just less than 1% of all non-institutionalized adults meet criteria

Narcissism	Machiavellianism	Psychopathy
disorder is named for the mythological figure Narcissus, who fell in love with his own reflection. According to Sigmund Freud, narcissism is a normal stage in child development, but it is considered a disorder when it occurs after puberty.	they behave in a highly manipulative manner."	for the disorder (Hare, 1996). The base rate of psychopathy is higher in institutional settings, with an estimated 15–25% of incarcerated individuals meeting criteria for the disorder.
Source: Encyclopedia Britannica/ Narcissism	Source: Psychology Today/Dark Triad	Source: ScholarPedia/ Psychopathy

Why is it important that you familiarize yourself with the dark triad? Let's allow the scriptures to answer this question for us.

- **Romans 16:17–18:** Now I beseech you, brethren, mark them which cause divisions and offenses contrary to the doctrine which ye have learned; and avoid them. For they that are such serve not our Lord Jesus Christ, but their own belly; and by good words and fair speeches deceive the hearts of the simple.
- **1 John 4:1–3:** Beloved, believe not every spirit, but try the spirits whether they are of God: because many false prophets are gone out into the world.

Hereby know ye the Spirit of God: Every spirit that confesseth that Jesus Christ is come in the flesh is of God: And every spirit that confesseth not that Jesus Christ is come in the flesh is not of God: and this is that spirit of antichrist, whereof ye have heard that it should come; and even now already is it in the world.

- **Proverbs 22:24-25**: Make no friendship with an angry man; and with a furious man thou shalt not go: Lest thou learn his ways, and get a snare to thy soul.
- **1 Corinthians 15:33**: Be not deceived: evil communications corrupt good manners.

The following information was taken from Frontier.com:

- **"Machiavellianism** is characterized by self-interest, lack of empathy, and interpersonal manipulation (Furtner et al., 2011). These negative characteristics may lead individuals with Machiavellianism to ignore the importance of the environment, and even choose the former in the trade-off between short-term benefits and long-term development. Specifically, on the one hand, individuals with Machiavellianism may try to gain advantage by any necessary means, without considering morality (Myung and Yun, 2017).
- **Psychopathy** is characterized by high impulsivity, thrill-seeking behavior, low empathy, lack of loyalty, and irresponsibility

(Boddy et al., 2010). Psychopaths are often attracted to power, prestige, and control (Deutschman, 2007), which leads them to focus on short-term benefits, maximize their wealth and power by making short-term decisions (Boddy, 2006), and achieve short-term economic benefits even at the expense of the environment.

- **Narcissism**. The main characteristics of narcissism are domination, expressionism, and exploitation, as well as superiority and entitlement (Lee and Ashton, 2005). Narcissism, as a multifaceted dimension of personality, captures the extent to which an individual has an inflated self-consciousness and is constantly focused on himself (Chatterjee and Hambrick, 2007). Narcissists tend to overestimate their creativity, abilities, and wisdom (Myung and Yun, 2017). They believe that social exchanges based on the concept of sustainable development provide less benefits and take longer, and have a desire for high returns in the short term. Therefore, they are more likely to choose to gain some immediate benefits through short-term actions than to achieve long-term benefits through sustainable development.

(Source: Frontiers.com/How Machiavellianism, Psychopathy, and Narcissism Affect Sustainable Entrepreneurial Orientation: The Moderating Effect of

Psychological Resilience/Wenqing Wu1, Hongxin Wang, Hsiu-Yu Lee, Yu-Ting Lin and Feng Guo).

One of the reasons you should want to learn more about, not just psychology, but dark psychology is so that you can place the right people in your circle, both intimately and intellectually. Additionally, you want to know who to remove from your circle and keep out of your circle. Understand this—people can and do change. I've had people walking closely with me who, without warning, changed. They grew cold, distant and completely unrecognizable. They suddenly became familiar strangers. I've sat them down to discuss what the problem could potentially be, and the answer has almost always been, "There is no problem" or "I'm just going through a lot right now." One thing you have to do is trust the Holy Spirit because, at times, people will attempt to remain in your life or remain in your intimate circle, all the while hosting a negative view of you. This view could have been shifted by a conversation they had with someone else about you, it could have been altered by an offense that they never discussed with you or it could be motivated by jealousy. Howbeit, a lot of people won't tell you what they're feeling when they are afraid of losing whatever benefits they believe that they stand to gain or they have been extracting while connected to you. And make no mistake about it—the longer you allow these people to remain connected to you or, at minimum, closely connected to you, the more time you'll waste learning a lesson that you shouldn't have to learn and the more trauma you stand to experience. You see, as you grow older, you learn that there's a shortcut to a lesson and there's a long journey that leads to that same conclusion. The shortcut is through wise counsel and by trusting the Holy Spirit. The long way starts when you get so distracted by a person's potential that you completely disregard that person's character. Satan loves to use potential to seduce God's people into a realm called deferred hope. Proverbs 13:12 (ESV) states, "Hope deferred makes the heart sick, but a desire fulfilled is a tree of life."

Nowadays, we are so focused on the trending topic of narcissism that we are completely ignorant to the fact that there are personalities out there that are far more sinister. This isn't to downplay the damage caused by narcissistic people; this is to say that we shouldn't be so focused on the alligator that we miss the tide. They both require our attention if we want to increase our chances of survival. Again, the objective of the Machiavellian personality, the narcissistic personality and the psychopath is all-on control, and please understand that control can be both covert and overt. The following information was taken from Psyche Study:

- **Overt Behavior:** The word 'overt' can be defined as something that is plainly apparent and openly displayed. The term overt behavior means just that. The observable behaviors such as walking, talking, laughing, which can be seen readily are categorized as overt behavior.
- **Covert Behavior:** Covert behaviors are unobservable actions which can only be deduced by oneself. A huge majority of psychologists reason

that behaviors are only eternal actions and behaviors which are observable. However, behavior is psychophysical in origin, and both internal and external world play equal role in occurrence of the behavior. Anything that brings alteration in the environment can be categorized as behavior, which means even when the actions are unobservable, they are behaviors. Examples of these covert behaviors are; perceiving, remembering, reasoning, thinking, creating and dreaming among many more. (Source: PsycheStudy.com/Overt Behavior/Covert Behavior/Praveen Shrestha).

The main reason you should familiarize yourself with dark psychology is so that you can protect your personal space and your heart. In other words, you don't want to end up hosting people in your life who are mentally and emotionally unstable. Believe it or not, most people who are tumultuous don't hide their narcissistic or abusive ways very well, contrary to popular belief. Some people would argue that the manipulators who managed to seduce and take advantage of them were almost undetectable in the beginning, but in truth, they can and will admit that they saw and dismissed quite a few red flags. Why is this? Because broken and toxic people have potential and, all too often, we fall in love with their potential. This causes us to either ignore just how damaged these people truly are. In some cases, we simply convince ourselves that we are competent enough to do the work needed to help these people become the amazing gifts they have the potential to become. This reminds me of a house my ex and I looked at while we were married. Our credit was in the pits and we'd finally come across a company that was willing to work with us. We ended up finding a house that was in a relatively decent neighborhood, but the house was in horrible condition. In truth, I think the house had already been condemned or it was on the verge of being condemned, but it had an incredible amount of potential, being as it is that the house was a dilapitated mansion. It was a two-story Victorian style home that was around four-thousand square feet in size, and the best part about it was the house was on the market for $32,000! This is because the house needed a lot of work done to it. Nevertheless, my ex was an off-record handyman; he could fix just about anything. He was an electrician so he could do the wiring, he'd worked for a flooring company, so he could replace the floors and I'm pretty sure he's had experience with dry-walling. We thought we'd be getting a steal of a deal and our mortgage would be no more than $300 a month. Of course, the bank refused to finance the house for two reasons; the condition of the house, plus the bank did not finance houses under $35,000. We were disappointed! But what neither of us realized was this— while he (the ex) had experience fixing the outward appearance of a building, he had no knowledge or experience with fixing the foundation, plumbing and a lot of the issues that are typically found beneath the surface. The bank understood that we were trying to undertake a project that was way out of our league, and the burden of that project would fall on them. The same is true for God. He sees every time we try to take on the arduous task of fixing another human being. Let's face it. Some people look and sound fixable, and when we see their potential, we start ignoring the fact that there are issues lurking beneath the surface that we don't have the ability to reach or repair. We have surface knowledge, but God knows what dwells in the darkness of man's soul. Going back to the cable guy story from 4.0, I thought I could briefly give the guy a mental tune-up. What I didn't realize was that beneath the surface, there were issues and demons that I was not yet equipped to deal with. Because of this, I found myself looking out the window of an X-Finity truck, praying that I wouldn't end up as fertilizer.

Dark psychology is what a lot of FBI and CIA agents familiarize themselves with because they are aware that they are going up against evil. How is it then that a lot of Christians are unaware of the fact that they are going up against evil every single day? With that said, here are ten characteristics of personalities found in the dark triad:

1. **Love bombing**: Love bombing is a tactic used by manipulators to accelerate the establishment of soul ties and to strength weakened soul ties. This wile is usually characterized by excessive compliments, flattery, attention, gift-giving and touching.

2. **Seduction**: Seduction is a method that is regularly used to trigger an emotional response, oftentimes through the use of sensuality. Sensuality has everything to do with your five senses: sight, touch, smell, hearing and taste. Contrary to popular belief, seduction is not always sexual, for example, a person can be seduced with food or with words. A seducer may say, "I'm cooking smothered steak,

asparagus and mashed potatoes, and then I'm going to wash it all down with a glass of red wine. After I finish eating, I'm going to light some candles and soak in my Jacuzzi while listening to jazz. And finally, I'm going to bathe myself in my favorite oils before going out on my patio to watch the stars." Notice here that the speaker is engaging all five of his or her senses, and whomever the speaker is communicating with is being enticed to join him or her.

3. **Strife:** Strife is like seduction in reverse. It's when you overwhelm the senses of a person through arguing, giving them the cold shoulder, withholding something from them or putting them on punishment altogether. If someone gives you the cold shoulder because you didn't do what the person wanted, the person is exhibiting signs of immaturity and emotional witchcraft.

4. **Lying:** Manipulators use lying so that they can control your perspective of them. This is why the moment you realize that someone is twisting your words or outright lying, it is a good practice to start writing down some of the things they say and place a time stamp and date on when they said it. The objective isn't to confront them and prove that they are liars (they already know this); the objective is for you to gather enough evidence (if needed) to sever ties with them. You see, we sometimes question others, but we interrogate ourselves, and we'd rather believe that we've misunderstood, mismanaged or misdiagnosed them rather than

believing that they are manipulative people. Or, we will romanticize their lies. For example, a woman may say to her best friend, "He just canceled our date because he's ashamed of the fact that he has no money. Instead of being honest, he said that he had to postpone our plans because he wasn't feeling good." In this, she's romanticized his lies. The truth of the matter is, he may have canceled their date simply because he has made plans with another woman or he simply didn't feel like going.

5. **Choice Restriction**: Manipulators tend to limit your choices in an attempt to control the outcome. A great example of this is when a woman, for example, is given a long list of properties for her and her fiance to consider, but in an attempt to control the narrative, the woman creates a short list from the long list before showing it to her fiance. In this, she shows him only the properties she is interested in. Another example of choice restriction is when a man only tells his love interest about a few of the restaurants in town, intentionally omitting the ones that he's not fond of in an attempt to steer the woman towards the ones he prefers. This gives her the illusion that she is being granted the ability to make a decision when, in truth, she's being manipulated and robbed of that ability.

6. **Reverse Psychology**: Similar to the tactic of choice restriction, the objective of reverse psychology is to promote one decision by discouraging another. For example, let's say that a mother recognizes that her teenage daughter is determined to date the town

rebel, and she knows that by discouraging her that her daughter will continue to have a crush on the guy. So, to sway her in another direction, she starts encouraging her daughter to approach the guy. This not only shocks and surprises her daughter, but it causes her to look at her love interest objectively. This is what we refer to as reverse psychology. The mother is not limiting her daughter's choices; she's controlling her daughter by making her question her choices. Another example of reverse psychology is when a person changes the direction of a conversation to deflect the attention or the blame from himself or herself. A great example of this is— Damien comes home at one in the morning, and his wife, Donna, is livid. The two argue and Damien suddenly asks his wife, "Why don't you like my mother?! This is what we really need to talk about!" Donna is confused. "Who said I don't like your mother?! I love your mother! Are you kidding me?!" Damien laughs. "Have you forgotten already?! I asked you to drop off a pound cake over to my mother's house on yesterday, but you refused! This is the second time you've refused to go over to my mother's house, and quite frankly, I'm getting tired of it! I've always treated your mother with the utmost respect, but for you to treat my mother like she's irrelevant is where I draw the line!" In this, you'll notice that Damien has shifted the conversation. The objective here is for him to cast his wife as the villain, all the while casting himself as the victim. This causes his wife to shift from being accusatory to defending herself and feeling guilty.

7. **Confusion**: This particular tactic involves either giving a person too many choices or twisting that person's words. Manipulators use confusion to make their victims question their sanity, their intelligence, their motives, their choices or the people around them. A good example of this is— Damien looks at his wife during their very heated argument and says, "Did you even call the flower shop back?" Donna is confused. "What flower shop?" she asks. "What are you talking about, Damien?" Damien shakes his head and walks away. "And you wonder what's wrong with our marriage," he says as he disappears into their bedroom. He appears to be brokenhearted and his voice cracks as he says to his wife, "I need space tonight. Either I'm sleeping in another room or I'm sleeping at a hotel, but I cannot sleep with you." Still confused, Donna asks, "Damien, what on Earth are you talking about? What flower shop?!" This is an example of confusion, and the objective here is, once again, to change the direction of the conversation and to shift the blame from himself to his wife.

8. **Sympathy/Guilt-Tripping**: Realizing that his wife is tired of his antics, Damien makes his way into the kitchen after spending an hour in the bedroom. On his way to the kitchen, he calls his sister, Ann. "How is she doing?" he asks Ann calmly. Standing just a few feet away, his wife, Donna, can hear his sister's voice, even though she can't make out what she's

saying. Moments later, Damien lets out an audible sigh. "I think we need to prepare for the worse, Ann. I'll break the news to Uncle Earl tonight." In this, Damien is still attempting to cast himself as the victim; the objective here is to not only garner sympathy from his wife, but to guilt trip her into thinking that she has been mismanaging his already ailing heart by questioning his whereabouts. Manipulators use sympathy to escape being held accountable for their actions. If they owe money to someone, they will use sympathy and guilt-tripping to avoid repaying their loans. Let's say that Donna divorces Damien and marries a guy named Frank. Like Damien, Frank is also manipulative and toxic, and on their wedding night, Donna asks Frank, "What's wrong? You didn't act too happy at the wedding. I understand that you may have been stressed, but I'm getting scared because you're acting like you don't want to be married to me. Did you have a change of heart?" Not wanting to be honest with his new wife, Frank decides to cast himself as the victim. "My stomach hurts," he says, as he turns his body away from his wife. "I think we should have gone ahead and went with the cake designer my Mom chose because I believe I have food poisoning from the cake you chose." Donna will have to pay close attention to her husband's words for the next few days to discover exactly what he wants of her and expects from her.

9. **Ex-Exaltation:** This particular wile is used on lovers and former lovers of narcissistic manipulators. An

example of this behavior would be Frank saying to his wife, "Tell me more about your ex, Derrick. Why did the two of you break up?" Understand that Frank's objective is to talk about his ex, Mya. Why does he want to talk about Mya? The answer is, Frank wants his wife to believe that Mya is his long-lost soulmate and his wife is just a fill-in. Not realizing what her husband is doing, Donna answers, "We talked about this before. I broke up with Derrick because his mother didn't like me, and he wouldn't defend me anytime she said something ugly about me. I didn't want to marry a man who wouldn't stand up for me." Lying on the bed next to his wife, Frank looks at the ceiling and smiles as if he's lost in some beautiful memory. "Yeah, that's similar to why Mya and I broke up. Don't get me wrong, we didn't have any interference from my mother, but her mother thought she could do better than me. I didn't want her to be at odds with her mother, so I ended the relationship. I'll never forget when I was getting in my car to leave her mother's house after breaking up with her. Mya made me cry, and you know it's not easy for me to cry. She ran after me when I started leaving and her brothers had to hold her back. I can still see her in the distance chasing my car and crying. I knew that I'd done the right thing, even though Mya and I had never argued. What's worse is, I didn't know that she was pregnant. Her youngest brother told me that Mya miscarried our son just three days after I left. I thought she hated me after that. That's why I was surprised when the Dean at my university told tuition, but he wouldn't tell me who did it. I knew it was Mya. I just knew!" Frank continues staring and smiling at the ceiling while his wife looks at him in dismay. Ex-exaltation is designed to make a person's spouse or love interest feel that their presence in their spouses' lives is but a chance encounter that should never have happened. The goal of this wile is to make the spouse or the love interest fight harder for the relationship and, in a sense, make them feel like they are the only barriers standing between their lovers and their true soulmates.

10. **Playing on Your Insecurities**: First, let's establish this fact—manipulators will rarely entertain confident people. Don't mistake what I'm saying; they will date a confident person, but only if that person's confidence is surface-level, while their insecurities are ground-level. What does this mean? Donna and Frank divorced after four years of marriage. In this, we've established that Donna was the victim, while Frank was the villain, but what if I told you that the toxic environment that Donna lived in for four years has changed the way she views the world—and men; would you believe it? Donna meets a guy by the name of Sanchez, and get this, unlike Frank, Sanchez is not a narcissist, nor is he a manipulator. He's a hard-working single father who simply wants love and happiness, and when he meets Donna, he believes he's met the woman he was supposed to marry. The problem is—Donna doesn't trust men. All the same, she believes that

Sanchez is too good for her. He's handsome, hard-working and well-spoken. Then again, there are a lot of women at their job who like Sanchez, but he only has eyes for Donna. Fearing that he'll mistreat and discard her like Frank and Damien did, Donna finds and focuses on one of Sanchez's insecurities. You see, Sanchez has three toes on his left foot. This birth defect left him really insecure about his feet, so Sanchez refuses to wear sandals or flip flops. One day, while at a local water park, Donna asks Sanchez to take off his shoes so that they can get on one of the water slides. What provoked Donna to make such a request? She noticed three women who kept looking at Sanchez and talking amongst one another. It was clear that the women all found Sanchez attractive, and even though Sanchez was intentionally ignoring the women, he was also enjoying the attention. "Let's get on the water slide," Donna says. "Take off your shoes." Sanchez is mortified. "Donna, you know why I can't get on a water slide," Sanchez counters. "What are you doing, Donna?" Donna looks over at the three women before looking back at Sanchez. "Oh my goodness, Sanchez! Nobody cares that you only have three toes! Get over it!" With that, the three women laugh and walk away while a humiliated Sanchez is left in shock. Realizing how evil his new girlfriend is, Sanchez ends their water park date, and after he drops Donna off at her house, he ends their relationship.

Understanding dark psychology would have helped Donna dodge a bullet by the name of Damien. Understanding dark psychology would have helped her to avoid Frank. Understanding dark psychology helped Sanchez to protect himself from a monstrous woman named Donna. Understanding dark psychology can also help you to navigate toxic work environments, social gatherings and any place that people tend to frequent. I always tell people this—it is silly to be ignorant of an enemy who so readily and consistently studies you! "Behold, I send you forth as sheep in the midst of wolves. Be ye therefore wise as serpents and harmless as doves" (Matthew 10:16).

THE LINK BETWEEN POLYTHEISM AND NARCISSISM

Polytheism can be defined as "the belief in or worship of more than one god" (Source: Oxford Languages). Wikipedia reported the following about polytheism:

> "Polytheism is the belief in multiple deities, which are usually assembled into a pantheon of gods and goddesses, along with their own religious sects and rituals. Polytheism is a type of theism. Within theism, it contrasts with monotheism, the belief in a singular God, in most cases transcendent. In religions that accept polytheism, the different gods and goddesses may be representations of forces of nature or ancestral principles; they can be viewed either as autonomous or as aspects or emanations of a creator deity or transcendental absolute principle (monistic theologies), which manifests immanently in nature (panentheistic and pantheism theologies). Polytheists do not always worship all the gods equally: they can be henotheists, specializing in the worship of one particular deity, or kathenotheists, worshiping different deities at different times" (Source: Wikipedia).

If you study Narcissistic Personality Disorder and you have an elementary understanding of demonology, you will safely conclude that what the world of psychology refers to as the narcissist, the church has been referring to as the Jezebel spirit for centuries on end. Remember Ephesians 6:12 says, "For we wrestle not against flesh and blood, but against principalities, against powers, against the rulers of the darkness of this world, against spiritual wickedness in high places." Jezebel, the woman, of course, was a Baal worshiper. Encyclopedia Britannica reported the following, "Baal, god worshiped in many ancient Middle Eastern communities, especially among the Canaanites, who apparently considered him a fertility deity and one of the most important gods in the pantheon." In this, you can see that Baal worshipers are polytheistic, meaning they worship multiple deities. Now, let's talk about Jezebel, the spirit. Revelation 2:20-22 reads, "Notwithstanding I have a few things against thee, because thou sufferest that woman Jezebel, which calleth herself a prophetess, to teach and to seduce my servants to commit fornication, and to eat things sacrificed unto idols. And I gave her space to repent of her fornication; and she repented not. Behold, I will cast her into a bed, and them that commit adultery with her into great tribulation, except they repent of their deeds." In this, Jesus was rebuking the church of Thyatira. What's interesting about this particular passage is that it was written around 95 AD; this was over 700 years after the death of Jezebel, the woman, so it goes without saying that the author was not talking about Ahab's wife and the former queen of Israel. In this, Jesus was talking about a spirit. The same spirit that inhabited Jezebel, the woman, was now masquerading itself as an angel of light in the church, and the church of Thyatira was tolerating it. Because of their passivity towards this spirit, the Lord said that everyone who commits adultery with Jezebel will be cast onto the same bed of sorrows and tribulation that served as her judgment seat. Please note that the word "adultery" is the natural equivalent of idolatry. What does this mean? People who link themselves to the narcissist through idolatry would find themselves experiencing the same hurts and judgments that Jezebel or, better yet, the narcissist is enduring. If you've ever been in a relationship with a narcissist, you can bear witness to the fact that being with them is complete and utter sorrow, but what you may not know is that the narcissist is judgment for believers who are polytheistic. But wait! Most Christians who've had their fair share of run-ins with narcissistic people will shout to the Heavens that they only worship one God, and that is the Most High God, YAHWEH. Nevertheless, if you get a broad understanding of polytheism, you'll soon come to discover that many believers worship:

1. Themselves. This is the very nature of sin.
2. Other people's opinions.
3. Heaven.
4. The wealth of the world.
5. Their lovers.

Sure, they are Christians and they believe that Jesus Christ is Lord, but remember, practitioners of polytheism worship multiple deities, and get this—Jezebel (the narcissist) is attracted to people who worship themselves. Another word for self-worship is sin, and while we all sin and fall short of God's glory, any sin that we refuse to repent of whenever we're given space to repent becomes an idol. Fornication is a prime example of such a sin. It is a form of self-worship.

This is why Apostle Paul, in 1 Corinthians 6:18, said, "Flee fornication. Every sin that a man doeth is without the body; but he that committeth fornication sinneth against his own body." In Exodus 20:3, God said, "Thou shalt have no other gods before me." In this, God is saying that we shouldn't have any other gods in place of Him or in front of Him. Does this mean that we can have other gods if we place them next to Him or under Him in rank? No. Jesus said in Matthew 6:24, "No one can serve two masters, for either he will hate the one and love the other, or he will be devoted to the one and despise the other. You cannot serve God and money." In other words, the narcissist or Jezebel spirit is judgment for idolatry. This is why the term "narcissism" is trending today. A lot of believers are unknowingly polytheistic; they worship themselves, they worship marriage, they worship houses, cars and wealth, and they worship the opinions of others. Consequently, they are within Jezebel's jurisdiction, and by this, I mean that the realm of thought they're in falls under a demonic principle, therefore, it is subject to a demonic principality. This is why we have to be transformed by the renewing of our minds. All the same, Jezebel has always been after God's prophets and prophetic people. 1 Kings 18:4 reads, "For it was so, when Jezebel cut off the prophets of the LORD, that Obadiah took an hundred prophets, and hid them by fifty in a cave, and fed them with bread and water." And understand this—the Jezebel spirit was on Earth far before Jezebel, the woman, was born. It is the same spirit that was in Cain, Potiphar's wife, King Saul, the Philistines, Haman and the list goes on. Why then was it given the name "the Jezebel spirit?" The best way I can answer this question is by using the logic behind retiring hurricane names. The following information was taken from weather.com:

> "Some Atlantic Basin hurricanes and tropical storms have had their names retired. Just as no New York Yankee will ever again wear No. 3 (Babe Ruth), nor will a Green Bay Packer ever claim No. 15 (Bart Starr), no future Atlantic hurricane will ever be named Harvey, Irma, Katrina, Maria or Sandy. Unlike an athlete's number, however, there is no celebration when an Atlantic name is retired from future use. Contrary to popular opinion, a committee of the World Meteorological Organization – not the U.S. National Hurricane Center – is responsible for the tropical cyclone name lists. Atlantic hurricane and tropical storm name lists repeat every six years, unless one is so destructive and/or deadly that the committee votes to retire that name from future lists. This avoids the use of, say, Katrina, Sandy or Maria to describe a future weak, open-ocean tropical storm" (Source: weather.com/Retired Hurricane Names: The Most Notorious Atlantic Storms Since 1954/Jonathan Erdman).

When a hurricane brings mass destruction and death to a region, that hurricane's name will likely be retired from use. The same is true for some demons. The demon in Jezebel was branded as the Jezebel spirit because of all the evils it's done. It's greatest handiwork and hallmark was bringing God's people into a covenant with Baal and killing off a large number of God's prophets. All the same, please understand that the Jezebel spirit does NOT mind people worshiping YAHWEH, contrary to popular belief, after all, Baal worship is a form of pantheism, which is "worship that admits or tolerates all gods" (Source: Oxford Languages). Why then did Jezebel kill God's prophets? Because in Baal worship, Baal has to be considered and worshiped as the supreme god. Many of God's prophets refused to turn to Baal worship when Jezebel was in power; this as a crime, in her faith, that was punishable by death. Of course, many of God's prophets embraced polytheism during that era. Some did it to save their own lives, while others did it because they were never committed to God in the first place. This is why God said to Elijah, "Yet I have left me seven thousand in Israel, all the knees which have not bowed unto Baal, and every mouth which hath not kissed him." The point is—whenever a person doesn't honor Matthew 6:33, which reads, "But seek ye first the kingdom of God, and his righteousness; and all these things shall be added unto you," that person will fall in dimension (spiritually and mentally) into Jezebel's lair. If that person happens to be a prophet or a prophetic person, Jezebel will take special interest in the individual because Jezebel has a thirst for the prophet's blood. This is to help you understand why you may have found yourself in the lap of the narcissist. Understanding why you fell into Jezebel's trap can protect you from falling into that same pit again.

Did you know that every deity requires a sacrifice? No, I'm not saying that there are other gods out there who are equal to God. I am saying that there are devils out there masquerading themselves as deities. What I've witnessed is believers using other believers and nonbelievers as calf. How so? Imagine this—a Christian woman desperately waits on God to send her a husband, not realizing that the delay she's experiencing in being found is due to the fact that she is outside of God's will. The problem is, she hasn't fully surrendered herself to God, so while she goes to church, serves in ministry and has a lot of Christian t-shirts, she is controlling, self-centered and heavenly minded. By heavenly minded, I mean that she idolizes Heaven or, better yet, she treats God as her sugar daddy. She wants to live in His house, but she does not want to embody His heart. Let's call this young lady Yolanda.

One day, Yolanda meets a man named Warren and the two of them hit it off really well. Warren is tall, dark, handsome, career-minded and somewhat successful. He seemed like the perfect catch, outside of the fact that he wasn't saved. "I believe in God," Warren once told Yolanda, "but I don't think I have to go to church and say hallelujah just to be a good person." After having waited for six years, Yolanda was desperate. The pool of single men at her church seemed to be shallow, and every time a decent guy got into that pool, the women at her church would darn near drown themselves trying to get the guy's attention. Yolanda once joked that this event looked like a piranha fest. One guy had even left the church Yolanda attended because, after having been delivered from porn addiction and lust, he'd said that he wanted to focus on the Word, but going to church every Sunday had proved to be a dance of sorts, especially after the benedictions had been said. "I would be stopped by women no less than eight times," the man joked. "They'd always be asking me to fix something, build something or give them something. After I started using the emergency exit to get to my car, that's when I realized that I needed to go to a different church!"

Yolanda has a close friend by the name of Laura. Laura and Yolanda have been friends for more than five years. They met at church while volunteering, and the two women have almost been inseparable ever since. Laura had been approached by Yolanda when the two women were doing set design one day, and this hadn't been the first time she'd approached her future best friend. She'd stopped her in the parking lot one Sunday, and a year prior to that, she'd given Laura a birthday gift, along with a prophetic word. But now, Yolanda was in a relationship and Warren was very demanding of her time. "I beseech you therefore, brethren, by the mercies of God, that ye present your bodies a living sacrifice, holy, acceptable unto God, which is your reasonable service" (Romans 12:1). Every deity requires an offering. Demonic deities require a sin offering, so remaining abstinent was out of the question for Yolanda the moment she exchanged numbers with Warren, and the moment Yolanda had sex with Warren, she'd become overly smitten with him. Her church attendance began to dwindle, but her interest in her friend, Laura, seemed to increase for a while. Whenever Yolanda wasn't around Warren, she insisted on being in the company of Laura. At first, Laura was happy for her friend, but she urged her to remain pure and to increase her church attendance, rather than decreasing it. Of course, Yolanda did not listen. She was more than determined to prove to Warren that he was quickly becoming her everything. And get this—Warren was a narcissistic male, and while he had never been diagnosed with Narcissistic Personality Disorder, he was definitely high on the spectrum of narcissism. What's worse is the fact that Yolanda continued to feed his narcissism, fattening up his ego and strengthening his pride one yes at a time. Since I've used an example similar to this before, what do you think will happen to Yolanda and Warren?

1. They'll likely marr j or have a kid, or both!
2. Yolanda will leave her church, but not before finding some reason to get offended with her leaders.
3. Laura will be Yolanda's fattened calf. This means that all the gifts, kind words and good deeds she'd done for her friend over the last few years can be summed up as her fattening up the calf for the sacrifice.

If you answered "all of the above," you are correct! Idolatry is both instinctual and spiritual, meaning people who practice it instinctively know what to do, especially when their deities are not satisfied. The moment that there is hardship between Yolanda and Warren, especially if that hardship won't d ssipate, she will instinctively look for something to sacrifice in an attempt to pacify the wrath of her god (Warren) and save her relationship. Lovers of narcissists do this to prove their love to their narcissistic partners. This is why a lot of us can testify to the fact that we've been discarded by a friend or two after those friends found themselves in relationships with not-so-sane people. While looking for a sacrifice, Yolanda will consider some of the things that Warren has complained about. If she has children and he's complained about her children, she will consider whatever remedies he's suggested. If he's complained about her church, she will go and find another church, or she'll stop going to church altogether. If he complained about her mother, she will find fault in her mother and use that issue to separate herself from her mother. If he's complained about Laura, she will behave coldly or rudely towards Laura before distancing herself from her. This is what modern-day polytheism looks like, and a lot of Christians are bound by it. I would dare to say that more than 50 percent of believers are unwittingly polytheistic. This is because we were told to seek God, and while this is good and right, Matthew 6:33 tells us to seek God FIRST! Yes, what we seek first matters!

One of the lessons to learn here is this—never bring polytheistic people into your intimate circle because, unbeknownst to you, you may be the proverbial calf that's being fattened for the upcoming slaughter. Never trust a person that God Himself cannot trust. Never give someone access to your heart when they have trouble guarding their own. Pray for the people in your life; encourage them and help them however you can, but the moment you realize that they are trying to place you on an altar as a sacrifice to someone they're entertaining, get off that altar and bid them farewell! You do this by:

1. Communicating with the person. Give the individual language for what he or she is doing. I have literally

told people, "I'm not lying on that altar. It's not necessary for you to sacrifice one relationship to save another." Of course, they didn't listen, but I didn't allow them to further harm or damage me for the narcissist's entertainment.

2. Place time, space and distance between you and that person. In other words, put that person in your intellectual circle and slowly or quickly spiral him or her out of your life.

3. Set, solidify and enforce boundaries with the individual. For example, I once told a former friend, "I no longer want to hear about Jake. I can't tell you who to date, but you said yourself that God told you to distance yourself from the guy. So, we can talk about any and everything else, but I'm no longer interested in hearing about Jake." Why did I set that boundary? Because the guy told her that he didn't want a relationship with her, she claimed that a prophet told her to back off, and finally, she said that God told her to back off. Nevertheless, she continued to entertain the guy, and she wanted me to listen to and celebrate her being outside of God's will. I refused to do this because I cared about her and I didn't want to become desensitized to the fact that Jake was playing games with her. Of course, she discarded me after I said what I said. Note: Don't forget to communicate your boundaries with the individual!

4. Ruminate the issue. Pray about it, get wise counsel and ruminate on the issue until you pull the wisdom out of it. Understanding what you've just

experienced will help you to heal a lot faster, and it will also help you to be more discerning when other people try to invite you into their intimate circles.

5. Study narcissism and the Jezebel spirit. Compare your notes. In other words, always study whatever it is that's been studying you! Never allow your enemy to know more about you than you know about him/her!

Whenever we dabble in polytheism, we are in the narcissist's neighborhood of thinking. This is why it is never good to play the victim. It is always better to look for yourself in every problem that you have; this way, you can come out of the problem, rather than trying to solve it. And finally, let's talk about how to seek God first. Study and apply the five pointers below if you want to grow your relationship with God.

1. **Repent.** Repent for idolatry, repent for your sins, the sins of your parents, grandparents and ancestors. This may sound silly, but it's truly effective. In the ministry of deliverance, we have people to do this before we proceed with deliverance. This addresses the iniquity in their blood and disallows the enemy to further accuse them.

2. **Study the Word daily.** Studying the Word of God daily is like talking with Him every day. In the beginning, you will have to date God, and then you'll court Him. During the dating phase, you'll have to force yourself to read the Bible, force yourself to go to church and force yourself to chase God. This is

because your flesh, at that stage, is stronger than your spirit, but remember, whatever you feed will grow; whatever you starve will die.

3. **Pray every day**. Do this several times a day. Don't just designate time with God before you retire for the night. Pray and talk with Him every day, several times a day. Don't be religious with it; tell Him everything! This includes your fears, your insecurities, your struggles ... everything!

4. **Wrestle down your idols.** For example, don't run to the internet when you wake up or hurriedly text your boyfriend/girlfriend. Put God first in everything. This means you should organize your life around your time with God, and not the other way around. In other words, get your life in order.

5. **Give up any and everything that puts a strain on your relationship with God**. This includes material possessions, jobs, ungodly relationships. Give God back His seat in your heart!

Downloading Kingdom Intelligence

There is a phrase that has changed my life astronomically in the last few years, and it is "I give myself permission." From there, I'll detail what I give myself permission to do, to not do, to feel or to not feel. This started around 2017 or early 2018. My mother was still on this side of eternity, and I was trying to find a way to convince her to take her medicine but, at the same time, I completely understood her position. She'd been battling with cancer on and off for years, and this time, she was tired of it all. She was tired of the chemotherapy, the doctors' visits, the hospital stays, the surgeries, feeling sick—she'd had enough of it all. So, when they'd diagnosed her with lung cancer, she pretty much had little to no fight left in her. I remember sitting in the doctor's office with her on the day of her diagnosis, and the doctor wanted her to go through another round of chemotherapy, but she was totally against it. She kindly but blatantly refused. The doctor suggested radiation. Again, she outright refused. My mother and I both preferred that she undergo another surgery, and we both expressed this to the doctor. This is because she'd had surgery a couple of years prior to this, and they'd successfully removed the cancer from underneath her rib cage. She'd healed well, and she didn't have to deal with being sick for months on end like she had when she'd undergone chemotherapy and radiation. The doctor wouldn't hear of it. She was more than determined to get my mother to undergo chemotherapy, so much so that she refused to sign off on her getting the surgery. The surgeon told us it was out of his hands. The only way he'd be able to set up a surgery date was if the doctor approved, but again, she wouldn't budge, despite what we wanted. Desperate to get my mother to do anything but have the surgery, the doctor then recommended chemo pills. "They'll turn your eyebrows white," I can remember her telling my mother, "But other than that, you should be okay." In the end, my mother insisted on the surgery, the doctor refused, and about a week or two later, my mom's chemo pills arrived in the mail. By this time, she'd returned to Mississippi. Of course, she refused to take the pills. Instead, she opted to combat her cancer by using the alkaline diet. An alkaline diet is a diet consisting of fresh fruits, vegetables, nuts and legumes. Partakers of this diet can also consume small amounts of meat and dairy products. It has been massively reported (via the internet) that an alkaline diet can reduce, treat and maybe even cure cancer. After doing days (if not weeks) of research, my mother decided that an alkaline diet was best for her needs, and while I supported her decision, I still tried to get her to take her medicine. Her medicine had arrived at my address in Georgia, and she repeatedly told me not to send it to her. "If I change my mind, I'll let you know," she'd say. My mother was passive, but she was also headstrong (strong-willed) in some areas. Once she made up her mind to do something, she'd do it. If she made up her mind to not do something, she wouldn't do it. At that time, I lived completely in denial and I'd allow the truth to have an occasional face-to-face visit with me, but we'd be separated by the glass wall I'd built around myself. I couldn't fathom the idea of losing my mother; that made no sense to me. She'd beat cancer so many times that I was convinced she'd beat it once again, but when the truth would stop by and pay me a visit, I'd have a moment of sobriety. My mother wouldn't be with me forever, and while I knew this, I didn't think she'd leave me so early in life. Howbeit, when I'd have those moments of clarity, I would stop and say, "I release myself from any guilt that would try to attach itself to me should my mother pass." I also began to release myself from feeling like I hadn't done enough to save her life. I'd especially have those moments after having long talks with her over the phone that felt more like arguments than conversations about her diet and the medicine she was refusing to take. Looking back, I now recognize that God was preparing me for my mother's transition, and He would give me those moments to sever ties with any ungodly thought and/or spirit that would try to attach itself to me. This worked. When my mother passed, I was able to grieve without the added pressures of guilt, regret and condemnation. Don't get me wrong—I've had my fair share of moments when I've thought about things I wish I'd done more, done differently or done better, but I don't blame myself for her untimely demise. This is what God used to teach me to loose myself from the cords of condemnation that would come upon me whenever an outcome was unfavorable. Howbeit, with favor comes pressure; with favor comes weight and responsibilities. Because of this, my days are incredibly busy. I design seals and logos for a living, I run a mentorship program, I write, publish and edit books, I create video trailers, I run a podcast and I have a beautiful dog, along with a myriad of household responsibilities, not to mention, I'm an elder and volunteer at my church. On any given day, I can find myself working or engaging with between 4 to 15 people who are either waiting on an order to be filled, inquiring about an order they want to place, needing counseling or working on something for me; the list is endless. While I count myself blessed, I have also learned to count myself in. What I mean by this is—there was a time when I felt like I was killing myself trying to make sure I took care of everybody's desires, demands and expectations. Spoiler alert: I failed repeatedly. I'd get a lot done and I'd make a lot of folks happy, but I would always fail somebody somewhere, and rather than focusing on what I had accomplished, I would obsess over what I hadn't finished. In other words, I pacified their impatience and criticized myself for not being able to empty my plate that day. I remember questioning whether I'd bit off more than I could chew when, in truth, I was just operating at ten percent of my potential (for that particular season). What this means is—God wasn't going to decrease my responsibilities, He desired to increase them, but how?! After all, the burdens He'd given me were already overwhelming. The answer is simple-by giving me Kingdom intelligence. What God taught me in that season was this:

1. To work smarter, not harder. He taught me to create systems that would allow me to accomplish more in a day's time.
2. When working with others, to ask myself, "Is this an emergency or is the client or student simply being impatient?" Don't get me wrong; I always meet my

deadlines, but sometimes, people want, for
example, their logos a lot faster (even though I
offer a twenty-four hour to three-day turnaround,
which is amazing and unheard of within itself). If
the client is being impatient, I've learned to politely
and professionally ask them for their patience.

3. To say no to some projects and offers. One of my
favorite adages or expressions is, "All money ain't
good money!" This is why I took my coaching
services down for more than a year. I needed to rest
from some of the demands placed on me by random
strangers so that I could focus on everything God
put on my plate.

4. To give myself permission to rest, to say no, to fail
and to disappoint others.

Luke 12:48 reads, "But he that knew not, and did commit
things worthy of stripes, shall be beaten with few stripes.
For unto whomscever much is given, of him shall be much
required: and to whom men have committed much, of him
they will ask the more." This is the trust of God! This is
the trust of mankind! In other words, the more we can do,
the more people expect us to do. This is why I had to learn
the importance of taking a break and saying no, not today,
not yet or never. Nevertheless, this is a beautiful problem
to have! What I mean is, the demand placed on my life
signals that God has granted me favor with Himself and
with mankind, and He's not only extended His trust to me,
but He has blessed me to win favor with mankind.

You cannot have Kingdom authority without first
downloading Kingdom intelligence. Think about it this way—

in the military, those who have greater rank also have a greater measure of knowledge and understanding, as well as a greater measure of trust and responsibility. And they aren't just given sensitive information and expected to retain it; they are given systems designed to help them retain and master the information they've been entrusted with. Within each system, you'll find protocols, policies and practices designed to help that system run smoothly and effectively. For example, I decided recently to reorganize a lot of spaces in my house. One of those responsibilities was bringing my new miniature shelves into the bathroom so I could better organize my makeup and everything that normally sits on the surface of the bathroom sink. I also had to make my way downstairs to grab a shelf that was three feet in height and carry it upstairs. As I was carrying the shelf, I began to think about systems and sub-systems. While the shelf would definitely play a vital role in helping me to organize my bathroom, it could easily fall prey to the system I was trying to eradicate. What I mean by this is—I realized that just neatly placing a bunch of things on the shelf would be a temporary fix to the problem. I needed something more sustainable. I thought to myself that I needed shelves or organizers to go on the shelves. This would allow me more space and it would also lessen the chance of me destroying my bathroom on those days when I'm in a rush to get somewhere. In this, I was identifying the need for sub-systems to support the main systems. I then thought about this fact—those systems would take time to build, and I'd learn to build them through trial and error. In other words, I was encouraging myself to be patient. I also encouraged myself to stay on top of what I was doing because, again, it is easy for an old system to eclipse a new one, thus rendering the new system impotent. This is how intelligence works! It sets one principle on top of another principle, thus building a throne for a principality to sit on. A principality isn't always demonic; I think we know this. When the principles of a person align with God's principles, God places a Godly principality (angel) over that person. This is why that individual can go into a region, an organization or an institution that has a demonic principality and not be affected by the cultures, legalities and curses affiliated with that space. For example, if you keep Jesus as your Lord and you serve Him, you could go to a city or town that has been completely taken over by evil spirits. You may notice that the people of that town are mean, seductive and prideful. You may also notice that some of the people who traveled to that space with you are slowly but surely bending to the winds or pressures around them, meaning they too are becoming mean, seductive and prideful. Howbeit, you won't conform to the temptations because you've repeatedly aligned yourself with Kingdom principles, therefore the principality assigned to your life will keep the demonic principality in that region at bay. How so? "So shall they fear the name of the Lord from the west, and his glory from the rising of the sun. When the enemy shall come in like a flood, the Spirit of the Lord shall lift up a standard against him" (Isaiah 59:19). Again, the standard is a boundary.

Kingdom intelligence centers itself around knowledge, but it does not limit itself to a particular dimension. Knowledge is the starting line, and while we'd love to believe that wisdom is the finished line, wisdom is another starting line. The finished line, however, is love, after all, God is love. "So now faith, hope, and love abide, these three; but the greatest of these is love" (1 Corinthians 13:13). Wisdom is having the insight of God, but love is the very heart and nature of God. It's when we can forgive effortlessly; it's when we don't just have to partner with Heaven, but we become an embodiment of Heaven on Earth. What I mean by this is—we come into alignment with God's will, God's Word and God's plan, understanding that we are little words of God, and who we connect ourselves with will determine the statements we make on Earth. You are a word and so are your friends. What statements are you making through those connections? If you are unequally yoked with unbelievers, the statements you make tend to cancel one another out with a conjunction. Oxford Languages defines the word "conjunction" this way: "a word used to connect clauses or sentences or to coordinate words in the same clause." Grammarly reported the following, "A clause is a group of words that contains a subject and a verb that have a relationship. This relationship is crucial; a clause conveys information about what that subject is or is doing, rather than simply being a random grouping of words." This is to say that, as a word of God, every relationship you form has a subject or purpose and a verb; this is the action or execution of that purpose. This is why you have to repeatedly take inventory of your relationships to see what they consist of and where they're headed, after all, the direction of any given relationship can change at any moment. All it takes is for one party involved to get hurt, offended or simply have a change of heart. A change of heart will always equate to a change of seasons. We don't ask ourselves the hard questions about our relationships because we tend to assume that if our intentions are good, our relationships are on the right track. This couldn't be further from the truth. Two can only walk together if they are in agreement (see Amos 3:3). This is why Kingdom intelligence is so important. It teaches us the importance of Godly connections and how to strategically connect ourselves with the right people, al the while quietly getting out of the reach of the wrong ones. For example, to be under siege means to be surrounded by enemies; right?! Understand this—a lot cf believers are under siege right now because they've surrounded themselves with the weapons that were formed against them, and they call these weapons their friends. This is because they've been taught to prioritize worldly intelligence over Kingdom intelligence. Who you allow in your inner circle makes a world of difference! They can determine how far you go, how high you go or how low you go in any given realm or season. It is a sad thing to see intelligent and anointed people chained to a bunch of broken and bound folks who have no desire to be free. The enemy uses the cords of toxic loyalty, ungodly beliefs, religion and expired revelation to keep them in bondage. He gets them to lock themselves into one-sided soul ties, demonic covenants, unrealistic expectations, ungodly family dynamics and a host of man-sized restrictions in an attempt to feel accepted. One tablespoon of Kingdom intelligence is potent enough to set them free, but they repeatedly vomit out the truth because the truth tastes bitter to a broken soul.

Who you have in your inner and close intellectual circles makes a huge difference. Think of it this way. What determines whether a neighborhood is a good one or a bad one? What are the characteristics of a good neighborhood? What are the characteristics of a bad neighborhood? The short answer is—mutual respect and a positive outlook of life. Let's examine them both.

- **Bad Neighborhoods:** My family and I lived in bad neighborhoods for the large majority of my childhood. What I remember most about these neighborhoods was that there was always a bully somewhere, crime was commonplace, you couldn't trust your neighbors and there wasn't a whole lot of honor being passed around. And because honor was in short supply, you had to demand something lower than honor, and that is respect. This is largely because bad neighborhoods sit atop the foundations of dishonor, disloyalty, toxic loyalty, anxiousness and pride; they represent the principle setters in those neighborhoods. Don't mistake what I'm saying—I'm not insinuating that *every* human who lives in a bad neighborhood is a bad person. I'm simply talking about what makes the neighborhood bad or the principles that the neighborhood was established on; then again, the neighborhood may have been good at some point, but had fallen subject to a set of ungodly principles at some point. For example, in a lot of crime-ridden areas, one of the principles is "snitches get stitches." This evil and demonic principle allows wicked people to do evil things without fear of human consequences. It silences or muzzles the people in the community out of fear of retaliation, and what it means is if you see someone committing a crime or know that someone has committed a crime, you have to lie to law enforcement. It forces innocent bystanders to partner with the people who make their neighborhoods dangerous by encouraging them to remain silent and pretend to know nothing. Some people would argue that it is poverty that makes a not-so-good neighborhood a seedy one, but the truth is, it is the condition of a man's heart that brings poverty. Poverty is usually comprised of dependency and co-dependency, which are both extensions of idolatry. Bad neighborhoods are also under the demonic ruler, Mammon, which is the demon associated with the love of money. Believe it or not, poverty is one of the principalities that is governed by Mammon.

- **Good Neighborhoods**: Good neighborhoods are often made of both honor and respect. This honor shows up in neighbors looking out for one another (neighborhood watch), treating the entirety of any given neighborhood as if it were their own, establishing a sense of unity and setting rules that all of the landlords or occupants of that area must abide by. Now, these rules aren't laws; they are principles that everyone must agree to in order to be considered a part of the neighborly fold. One such principle, for example, is keeping the yards manicured. Another unwritten rule is noise ordinance, wherein residents agree to keep their music and every other noise low so that their immediate neighbors are not interrupted by those sounds. Another rule or principle is tidiness. It's making sure that you don't have trash, debris or broken vehicles strewn across your yard. Next, there's upkeep of the home, and lastly, it's only inviting people to your home who understand and respect the unwritten laws of the land. These are the threads that make a neighborhood a good one.

This is to say that good neighborhoods aren't good because they are comprised of high-wage earners; they are good because the people come together in unity. "And the LORD said, Behold, the people is one, and they have all one language; and this they begin to do: and now nothing will be restrained from them, which they have imagined to do" (Genesis 11:6). All the same, bad neighborhoods aren't bad because they are comprised of low wage earners; they are bad because their foundations are established on dishonor. Now, consider yourself a house, and your neighborhood is comprised of the principles and principle-setters that make up your life. The people in your intimate circle are your close neighbors, and the people in your intellectual circle make up the rest of your neighborhood. Knowing this, would you say that your life is nestled in a good neighborhood or is it time for you to move? Kingdom intelligence is not just knowing that you have to move, it's also knowing not to settle. You see, you will get offers and opportunities, but you have to be okay with being alone (if

God calls you to a season of silence) until you're healthy and whole enough to walk closely with the people that God intends to bring into your life. Understand that your paths will cross as you are journeying in Christ, growing in the things of God and allowing the scabs of pride and ignorance to fall away from you. In many cases, your paths will even merge; when two paths merge, close friendships are formed. When they cross, friendships and fellowships are formed. I've learned to not devalue the fellowships simply because they didn't blossom into friendships. Every person in your life functions at his or her greatest capacity when that person has the space or grace needed to grow. I have had people in my life that I have complained to God about, mostly because they were pulling on my platonic side while showing me their sisterly side. I felt robbed, used and stupid because I felt like they were extracting an incredible amount of friendship benefits from me while giving me their bare minimum. I labeled them as "users" and prepared to evict them from my life. That is until the Lord addressed me. He helped me to understand that one of my best faces is friendship; this is because I haven't allowed the failed relationships of my past to influence my future. I've healed and matured in those areas, therefore, I am at a high peak of production in those areas. On the platonic side, they weren't necessarily where I was, so they showed me the productive sides of themselves. The problem with this was that their productive sides didn't bear as much fruit as my productive side. Here's what the Lord taught me:

1. Allow people to pull on your friendship side from time to time so that they can see what a true friend

looks like, but don't allow them to become dependent on you in that area. Show them your sisterhood/brotherhood face or whatever side of you that they need, and not necessarily the sides they keep pulling on. Wherever you are at the peak of your production, you will have a lot of people pulling on that side of you. Sometimes, you have to disappoint them by not allowing them to readily access that dimension or extract the benefits from that dimension.

2. Sow the right seeds in the people God connects to you. Don't bash them, encourage them. And stop sowing seeds in areas where there is no light to grow those seeds. By this, I mean that the individual has not submitted that area to Christ. Speak life into that area; encourage them, educate them and empower them, but if they insist on walking in darkness in those areas, you have to disassociate yourself from that particular side of them. For example, if I keep talking to a friend of mine about her reckless spending, and I point her to a few money management books and courses, I've done my job. If she doesn't do anything with what I've shared with her, my job is to close myself off to that side of her. So, if she starts talking about finances, I'll change the subject but not before reminding her that we are not friends in that area, therefore, to protect our relationship, it is better that we avoid talks about money. I'd recommend that she get herself a financial advisor, and then I'd change the subject. In other words, I'd spin around

and show her another facet of me, instead of allowing her to pull on my financial face.

3. Establish a firm set of boundaries, and then communicate those boundaries with the people in my life. After this, answer any questions that they may have, and finally, take on the arduous task of repeatedly enforcing those boundaries. Sometimes, enforcing a boundary is simply reminding someone that an area of your life is off limits to them. For example, I told a former friend of mine that I would no longer be discussing money with her, nor would I continue to loan money to her. This was to protect our friendship. She agreed. Nevertheless, because she was filled with voids in the financial arena of her heart, it was only a matter of time before she started hinting around about her financial situation. She asked for prayer, letting me know that her lights and cell phone were about to be disconnected. I felt a strong pull on me to loan her money yet again. She didn't ask for it; she simply pulled on that side of me by grabbing my heartstrings. I had to resist the temptation to rescue her; this was so she would mature in that particular area. I felt bad when her lights were disconnected and she said that she was sitting in the dark, but I knew that I was doing the right thing because she was a reckless spender who kept putting her bills off to finance her feelings. In this, I learned that the boundaries I'd set were strong enough to keep her from plowing through them, but I also had to set and solidify principles that would prevent me from disregarding

my own boundaries.

4. Fruit is meant to be eaten. It is unwise for me to be productive in an area, and then shut that area off. That's like having an apple orchard that's producing a lot of apples, and then shutting that orchard off because the orange grove next door is in a different season. Sometimes, you have to help others until they are strong enough to stand on their own two feet, but remember, it is unwise to help people who refuse to help themselves.

5. A farm is comprised of well-manicured trees, plants and vines. A farm could easily become a forest if the people around you aren't intentional about putting or keeping their lives in order. If the people around you are like wild trees, thus creating a forest around your farm, you will have to deal with the wild animals (demons and demonized people) that creep into your farm from those forests. This is why you have to be careful in regards to who you bring close to you.

Don't forget to give yourself permission to want better for yourself. Give yourself permission to say no, not now, not yet or not ever. Give yourself permission to heal. Give yourself permission to grow. Give yourself permission to not be okay at times. Give yourself permission to disconnect from any and everyone who is not producing good fruits in your life. Give yourself permission to be great! Your objective is to continuously grow your relational or Kingdom intelligence; this way, you can extract all of the benefits of being a Kingdom citizen.

Sure, you may have been hurt, taken advantage of and misunderstood, but this was because God wanted to grow your intelligence in His Kingdom. With greater intelligence comes greater rank, and with greater rank comes greater responsibilities. I can truly say this—I am in awe of what God has done in my life relationally. I have some of the most amazing people in my intimate and intellectual circles, and get this—some of them are my friends, while others are not, and that's okay! They aren't my enemies; we are just not intimate or close enough to label one another as friends, but some of them have been greater blessings to me than my friends have! In this, I have learned the power of gratitude, and more than that, I have learned how the strategic placement of people in my life has allowed me to soar above my potential to reach heights unimaginable! This is because they encourage me, push me, support me and love me, and I try to give them more than what they've given me in return. This is the only competition I engage in!

List the people in your life, and determine what circles they fall in. Also, be sure to create a separate document listing the benefits, allowances and restrictions associated with each circle. And don't forget to overly communicate with the people in your life. Finally, never try to extract a blessing that you refuse to be! This is how you grow your relational acumen; this is how you increase in Kingdom intelligence! Sure, the weapons that are formed may not be able to prosper, but this doesn't mean that they won't function. All too often, we find ourselves healing from heart wounds that could have been prevented had we taken the time out to test the spirits, do inventory of our relationships and pray for and about the people in our circles. Remember, life isn't what you make it, it's what you allow it to make you! Don't stop here. Continue to grow your relational acuity so that you can be the blessing you want to attract, and last but not least, don't forget, it is not in your best interest to always put your best face forward. Give people the side of you that they need, and not necessarily the side of you that they want or the side of you that's the prettiest. If this causes some people to exit your life, you haven't lost anything. If anything, you've simply given yourself permission to remain sane! All the same, God is just giving you room to grow! Those people were siege walls in your life; when they left you, the walls of bondage fell one level and layer at a time! We have to stop despising deliverance when it doesn't look the way we think it ought to look. We all want love and security, and the paths that lead to these two realms can sometimes be lonely. Being lonely is not the same as being alone, after all, God is with you. All the same, your path will merge with the paths of righteous people as you continue your journey. Some of those paths will be continuous, while others will fork off and be short-lived. Some people will go all the way with you, while some will wander off into the wilderness because of temptation. Some people will wander away from you, all the while remaining on the God-path. Your path in Him was simply different than their paths. Your job is just to keep healing and moving forward in Christ until you reach the end of your potential. This is when the power of God takes over, and you'll find yourself moving in miracles, signs and wonders, surrounded by people who give you the space to be who you are! That's the miracle that you've been wanting and waiting for; that's the power of relational acuity!

Lastly, don't beat yourself up when people fall away from you or walk out of your life simply because you chose Kingdom intelligence over worldly intelligence. Most people don't mind remaining stuck in the dungeons of mediocrity and perversion, and they are only loyal to those regions of thought. This means that while you were in the low place with them, they appeared to be loyal to you when, in truth, they were loyal to a set of principles. You will discover this to be true the moment you abandon those principles. Nevertheless, God will bring you better friends and companions as you journey with Him. And trust me when I say—if you refuse to quit on this journey, you will truly understand just how powerful you are in Him and He is in you! You will find yourself at the top of the mountain helping others to find their way through the many levels of change. This may seem like a long and arduous journey, but I can truly say this—it's so very worth it!

You got this because God's got you!

www.ingramcontent.com/pod-product-compliance
Lightning Source LLC
Chambersburg PA
CBHW072340090426
42741CB00012B/2856